The Lord of the Absurd

The Lord
of the Absurd

Raymond J. Nogar, O.P.

HERDER AND HERDER

1966
HERDER AND HERDER NEW YORK
232 Madison Avenue, New York 10016

Imprimi Potest: Gilbert J. Graham, O.P.
Provincial
Nihil obstat: Benedict Endres, O.P., S.T.D.
Augustine Rock, O.P., S.T.D.
Censores deputati
Imprimatur: Cletus F. O'Donnell, J.C.D.
Vicar General, Archdiocese of Chicago
January 21, 1966

Library of Congress Catalog Card Number: 66–22608
© 1966 by Herder and Herder, Inc.
Manufactured in the United States

what's beyond logic happens beneath will:
nor can these moments be translated: i say
that even after April
by God there is no excuse for May

e. e. cummings

Contents

The Lord of the Absurd

I. CHICAGO

The Passing of the Picture People

But for two people, the lecture hall had now cleared. I gathered my papers together and prepared to leave. Then they rose slowly, those two figures, and came forward. They were little old ladies who walked with the air of the school teacher, shy, reserved, yet professional. As they approached, they conferred with each other, as if to make the final plan for action. The spokesman addressed me: "Father, we enjoyed your lecture very much tonight; we have attended all four of your series." "Thank you, kindly," I replied, wondering what might be on their minds. "We followed your proofs for the fact of evolution very closely, Father, and they were clear and forceful." I nodded with appreciation. "But we were wondering, Father, now that everyone is gone," and here she made sure that no one had reentered the room, "if you would tell us what you really think. Do you really think that evolution is a fact?"

Lecture at the University of Illinois Medical School, 1964 "On the Fact of Evolution"

Speaking, whether in private or in public, is a special, unique mode of human existence. There is a sense in which a person can think and feel and love without being able to communicate these acts. But speaking is not merely an "instrument" of man's existence. A man can exist for a long time, perhaps almost all his life, in a kind of dormant, vegetative state. Until he speaks, he does not exist as a man. Only speech

11

allows the spirit free flight. Only in speech does a man transform his universe by his very own personal creative act. In his speech, you discover the man; in his speech, a man discovers himself.

It has been said that the eyes are the windows of the soul. But they are picture windows for people who want to look out upon the cosmos and see shapes and colors and objects in motion. But the ears are the doors of the spirit which open up to other persons and allow them to come into our life and us to go out to them. When I was a very young boy my father used to tell us a story as he rocked us to sleep. As the shadows lengthened, the objects faded from view and the sounds began to take over. The rocker had a special squeak which I remember to this day. But it was the sound of my father's voice which brought the drama home to me. With eyes closed, my ears registered the tones, the emotions, the interior personality of the story-teller. My father would then, finally, come inside, and a whole new world would emerge—one which I could not recapture in the morning no matter how hard I tried. Nor was my father the same; a fact which bewildered me more than once. In those words of his story, he lived and I lived and the people of his story lived. Outside the story, we had an existence, but it was quite other.

This is not a novel observation. St. Paul speaks of "hearing the word of God" and the necessity of preachers (not writers) to preach the word "in season and out of season" that men might believe. Special place was given to hearing so that the full force of personal communication could convince and not merely inform. Thomas Aquinas gives personal speech precedence over the written word when he explains how it was fitting that our Lord should have taught by word of mouth but not by writing. Speech filled with the power of personality, love and understanding directly enters the hearts of the hearers. But the power of speech has to be discovered anew today because of the complications of communication and the admixture of artifice and noise which has depersonalized much of human relationships. Human speech does not merely *do* something to a person; it *is* something of the person speaking and the person hearing.

Writing can become a monologue remaining entrapped within the egotism of the writer, and monologue is by nature untidy and filled with illusions. It is speaking with others which allows the egotism of the spirit to be cracked open and penetrated by the understanding and love of another. This dialogue is the only hope of correcting our myopic visions, our illusions, and the essential untidiness of our thought. Speaking with others, breaking out of a perpetual monologue, is a safety-valve against madness, the pathology of playing over and over the same broken record. Being alone, thinking alone, loving alone and speaking alone is very dangerous, and a man has to have an overriding excuse to be thus habitually occupied. *Genesis* revealed the mind of God on the point: "It is not good for man to be alone." If the cloistered contemplative did not center his life on spiritual dialogue, higher than mere human communication, his existence would be fragmentary and intolerable. Monologue is always a bit incongruous. The "strong, silent type" may be an eccentric whose hidden conversation is a mystery to be plumbed or a pa-

13

thology to be pitied. His conversation may be with the gods; then again, he may be neither strong nor silent. He may be incessantly talking to himself.

Lecturing began for me as a job, a work to be done. It belonged to the active workaday world, like driving a bus or running a printing press. Now lecturing is an element of my existence, like breathing and loving. In a real sense, for me to be, to live, is to speak. What has happened to bring about this change?

The first time I seriously reflected upon this matter was after a lecture in Chicago on the "fact of evolution" to a group of scientists, largely biologists and medical people. I was attempting to explain the difference between a "fact" in theology and a "fact" in science in order to show why the theologian does not ordinarily give so great a degree of credence to evolutionary theory as does the average scientist. To the theologian, I asserted, the evidence for evolution established it as highly probable; to the scientist, the fact of evolution is incontestable. One must understand, I went on, how and in what manner the fact of evolution is not "demonstrated with certitude." After the lecture, two young married geneticists came up and congratulated me on the interesting piece of dialectical side-stepping I had had to do to establish my position. Then one of them made an observation I was to hear again. "You know," he said, "you draw such fine lines of argumentation in this matter to explain how evolution could be only probable, but we are sure that *subconsciously* you think evolution is unquestionable. The conscious reasoning you go through is fascinating, *but it is not you.*" At the time, I wrote the incident off as an amateur attempt at psychological probing, but even then I had to acknowledge the large element of realism in the observation. *I did think,* then, that the fact of evolution was incontestable, even by the theologian. My reason for laboring the point was an extrinsic one: to defend the theologian's proneness to ask for too much in scientific matters, an anxiety which has always made him unduly suspicious about evolution.

Some months later I was lecturing in New Orleans at Xavier University and we were discussing some aspect of my lecture at a luncheon. Suddenly, a young lady from the department of literature, to whom everyone affectionately referred as "Winnie," spoke out. "There is a difference of day and night," she said, "between your lectures on evolution and your book [*The Wisdom of Evolution*]. In your book you are terribly logical, so excruciatingly structured in your thought. But in your lectures, you move on an almost intuitive, dramatic plane. In your book, you paint a picture; in your lectures, you tell a story. When you lecture," she went on, "I believe you are in it, but in your book, I cannot find you anywhere."

Well, there it was again. But that was the first time I had heard it put quite that way: the difference between painting a picture, a view of things, and telling a story, dramatizing reality. The response of the reader to a picture of reality and of the playgoer to a role in a play are quite different. In the drama, the story told, a person identifies himself with other persons. The response to a world-view and picture of reality which has its order, its detail in color, shape and motion, is an aesthetic experience of another, somewhat detached nature. It has to be admitted that the contrast between painting a

15

picture and telling a story, when describing my writing and my lecturing, is not altogether felicitous. Identifying a world-view with painting and the unfolding of the life situation with drama has serious limitations. A good painting is not merely a photographic image, nor is it impersonal; it has a dynamic, living quality which grows in aesthetic depth with the passage of time. Bad drama can be stultified by artifice, "play acting" and sentimentality to the point of becoming impersonal and lifeless. Granting this, it remains true that a picture, painted or otherwise, represents persons and events with a finished image, whereas the dramatic event is essentially epigenic and unfolding. In a picture, somehow the integral parts are all there; in a story, a drama, everything is developmental. Until the last curtain goes down, theme, plot and characters unfold in such a mysterious way that the viewer does not know "what is coming next." In this way, I think that it is correct to say that the dramatic event engages you personally, whereas the response to the picture of reality is somewhat more detached.

I began to notice this enormous difference in the response to what I wrote and what I said in my lectures. For years, my closest friends had read what I had written and had responded in a detached and impersonal way. In fact, they found nothing to believe in, nothing to comment upon, nothing of me. But put those same thoughts before an audience in a lecture and the opposite was true. In the written word, the result was an impersonal view; in the spoken word, the result was a deeply personal drama, a story in which both I and the listener played a role.

It was then that I realized that there were two modes of

human existence, two kinds of people: *picture people* and *drama people,* depending upon how they looked upon life. The first looked for a picture of things in order, a cosmic and personal world-view; the second looked for a drama unfolding. The first were restless until they felt that they had grasped something timeless, some eternal verity, and had placed themselves securely into changeless order. The second were impatient and distrustful until they found themselves in the space-time story of reality unfolding, a drama in which they had a part. They wanted to be involved; dynamically identified with all reality. But the picture people wanted just the opposite: detachment, escape from the effort and effect of the sorrows and joys of biographical and temporal existence. In writing, I could achieve the latter; but when I began to speak, reality began to move, and I could not stop or even slow down the drama. The subject might be the same but the mode of existence had changed. That meant that the truth itself was not the same, for a new facet of reality had been explored. For the spoken word is alive in a way that the written word is not, and its transforming effect is far more creative and moving and personal. It penetrates more deeply, and mysteriously carries the listener along into a new realm of being, one in which neither the speaker nor the listener can hold back a part of his existence.

When I say that neither the speaker nor the listener can hold back a part of his existence, I especially mean the speaker, the one who fashions the word. For in all these lectures, something was happening to *me*. I began as a teacher, one who professionally leads a learner to the sources of understanding and knowledge. Words, for me, were in-

17

struments to convey my ideas, tools by which I attempted to put into somebody's head what was in mine. But as I lectured week after week in the universities across the country, I began to notice that the moment I mentioned key words like "evolution," "Adam," "Darwin," "near-men," "the Bible," there tumbled in upon the minds of the listeners at an alarming rate a multitude of incongruous and troublesome thoughts. It was not simply a matter of getting the relationship of science and theology straight. I knew that the man who rose to ask questions and comment upon the lecture was personally caught up in a very important and terribly confused amalgam of "Darwin, Bible, atheism, religion, creation, Huxley, God and near-men." He didn't want a picture; he wanted the drama to unfold, and he knew that he had a part. But by the same token, I also knew that I had a role in that drama, and that I was entering into an existence in which I was not too sure what my role was. I found myself struggling to comprehend the *nuances of his thought,* the life of his words, to share his being which has been intruded upon by something I had said.

I began to understand what Henri Delacroix meant when he said that "the word is created each time it is uttered." I had spoken something that I had written many times, like, let us say, "Moses lived in the fifteenth century before Christ and could not possibly have known of the Pithecanthropus family which lived about 800,000 years before his time." In a book, a statement like this could be managed with a paragraph of careful chronology based upon paleontology and archaeology. No trouble. But when a man whom you never have seen before stands up and utters anxious sounds from

18

the depths of his religious being about this statement, you hesitate as before the brink of a canyon. This is no trifling business, entering into the personal drama of a man whose troubled existence has just been created by the words you have spoken.

What had hitherto been my problem had now become *our problem,* one of a shared existence which would leave us both altered. I discovered that I was no longer the pedagogue; I was a travelling lecturer walking into the hearts and souls and lives of others. A new dimension had changed my own existence, the necessity of understanding the drama of the listener's life and responding to his queries, his anxieties, his bottomless search—all of which was ultimately moral and religious. I began to question the adequacy of my own knowledge, my own understanding, my own sympathy and my own responses. I began to change. I should say that the communication of the word, the community of speech, in the proper sense of personal interchange, had begun to re-form and to re-create me. As I emerged from each lecture and each discussion, I found that I was a changed man. Not only was I changing from a picture man to a drama man, I was constantly changing my role in the drama.

The consequences were tremendous. In the first place, I found that public lecturing had become a necessity for me. The reason was not that I had to have something to do, like avocation therapy, any more than a woman finds that she needs marriage in order to occupy her time. Lecturing had become, not a work, but an existence, one in which I was daily discovering the world, myself and the way things are. I had not found it elsewhere, neither in the religious profession of my life which was "made to order," nor in my teaching which was "made to order," nor in those things I was called on to represent which were "made to order."

Make no mistake. I am not repudiating any of these pre-fabricated orders of existence as not necessary to my very being, any more than a child can cast off his youth as he becomes a man. We are constantly discovering our deepest vocation, and it is not uncommon that what at one time seemed our Joseph's coat later becomes a castoff, even a symbol of betrayal. The cicada must burst through its nymphal encasement before it can begin to fly.

A man needs more than a commitment, a life-partner, a business, a profession, a way of life, a daily schedule of appointments, a job. He needs a deeply creative, free and personal encounter with the way things are, and until the last ties are severed whether to things, to persons, or to institutions, he cannot discover who he is. It may be in some way true to affirm that "a fool in his heart says there is no God," but Max Scheler was uttering a profound personal truth when he declared that he first breathed a sigh of relief when he discovered that there was no God. He was no longer chained by an intolerable oppression. He was mistaken about the alleged oppression, but he was no fool. God is in Himself loving and liberating and the only promise of joy a man may ultimately have, but He may be presented to the spirit of a man as the oppression of oppressions. Such is the mystery of atheism. I began to grasp how necessary these discussions were to my entire religious life of teaching and writing. Lecturing was the open door, for me, to the way things are. My speaking, for the first time, revealed the heart of existence to me.

What I am saying about the spiritual reality of the human word, the existence of man through his speaking, applies equally to private speech and conversation. But the breakdown of personality, of the intimate bond of personal love, of the structure of society and nation and world community is basically an impediment of speech. In speaking, men become themselves fully, transform their realities and share their realities with the community. This is the way that understanding and love become one; the solidarity of the human spirit is built upon speaking. Human love, value, marriage, religious vow, heroic involvement, science, art and victory over death are all accomplished through speaking the word. Lovers transform each other's worlds by their words; when they stop speaking, love is dead.

Manuals of rhetoric commonly divide the subject of communication into departments: the personality of the speaker, the audience, the message and the style. But the spiritual activity of speaking cannot be so divided without some detriment to the reality of spiritual communication. In speaking, I came to realize, the speaker, the listener, the content of the word and the spectrum of gestures, affection and manner constitute a single organic whole. To the experienced lecturer, the difference between "giving a talk" and lecturing is great. I used to carry around "talks" in my brief case, as though lecturing were a matter of plucking out a manuscript and reading it aloud. Indeed, this can be done, just as a play can be "put on." But the transforming effect of speaking, in its most creative phases, calls forth much more interpersonal existence, one in which the speaker, the listener and the word are caught up in a drama of human experience which reinterprets the world and gives directions to an existence which otherwise would remain utterly senseless.

With each speaking engagement, I sensed consequences which ran deeper and were even more serious. The cosmos, the world of man, was not as I had pictured it for almost half a century. If speaking were the spirit of understanding and love by which men were calling into existence the intrinsic reality of the cosmos and the world of human value, then without question, the old world orders were crumbling. If our life space is not a vast mute vacuum but a territory in which each word is a creation and each creation is a definition of a role in the human drama, then the world of the Greeks, of the Schoolmen, of Galileo and Newton, of Descartes, Kant and Hegel was over. We may have discovered the universe and mankind through the established language of former ages, just as the child discovers reality through the traditions of his peers. But the adolescent discovers *values* in another iconoclastic and painful way, by revolting against the picture of the past and substituting the drama of his own personal existence.

Tradition, so necessary to human life and peaceful existence, ever tends to reduce the drama of life to a picture of an ideal world-view. But a man must ask himself, if he is to take hold of his own destiny, what if there were no such established picture, no such organized world-view of existence? What would I do? What would I be? What if there were no Church; would I find God? Would I even seek

Him? What if there were no established law; would I be just, give love, live discreetly? What if there were no organized cult, no Mass, no rubrics; would I worship? If there were no "*Adoro Te,*" would I sing a hymn of praise?

Or would my day collapse into a vacuum of drab, passive, aimless endurance? This is the issue. The greater part of our day is structured economically, socially, morally and religiously. Expectation is upon us from without like a vise and a yoke. And it is a blueprint which is largely designed by others—our family, our culture, our Church. Chaos would follow if it were not so. A man had better think twice about uprooting moral and religious traditions and customs: the revolutionary has always been judged worthy of death for "destroying the peace." Socrates was executed for what seemed to be moral revolution, and Christ was often accused of this crime of subverting sacred legal customs. Yet the issue confronts every adult today. In the existence of my few years upon this planet, do I have a role to play in a significant drama? Is there room for my unique, perhaps erratic emotional and intellectual talents on the stage of this drama? Is it meaningful to say that there is a time and a place for my unique freedom and personal creativity? Or must I be content to fit into a slot, like a piece of cardboard in a jig-saw puzzle?

With each lecture discussion, it became clearer to me that whether the subject was the future of man or the revelation of Christ, the drama people were replacing the picture people.

Thomas Aquinas had a second reason why it was not fitting that Christ write down his teaching for posterity. His interpretation of reality, the Divine revelation of the meaning of existence, was too mysterious to be written. It had to be lived, to be acted out, as it were, in the presence of those who could personally understand with love. This was a disturbing thought for me. What of all those formulas of the Christian world-view? What of all those blueprints of theological orientation into which the Christian cultures had attempted to assimilate the arts, the sciences, and the philosophies of each new age? Were they adequate to bring the teaching of Christ into the life of mankind? Or were they highly limited systems which were destined to fall short in touching men's lives with Christ's mysterious love?

My work was one of interpreting the problems of evolution in terms of ultimate meaning and human relevance. If Christ could not convey this with a picture, a world-view that could be systematically formulated, but had to live this meaning out in the drama of His life, how could it be otherwise for us today? Has the revealed meaning of our lives become less mysterious? Could it be that we are forcing Christ into the kingship of an order which He refused to acknowledge as His own before the very Jews who were awaiting His coming? Could it be that we are forcing Him into a cosmic picture which He refused to acknowledge as His own before the Greeks, a refusal which was sheer folly to their wise men? Can the meaning of the Cross, the only symbol of lordship which Christ would acknowledge as His own, be expressed in a doctrinal world-view, a picture of reality; or must that meaning of the Cross, of necessity, be lived out in a personal drama?

Everywhere in America and Europe, the spirit of man is speaking strange words: words about the illusions of former philosophies, the uselessness of cultural baggage, the irrelevance of old world-pictures and set ways of the value-systems of yesterday. Men have passed from naïve confidence to doubt and denial. Agnosticism and atheism are not just name-tags for a handful of renegades, they are essential conditions of the spirit of our times. Men are speaking, and speaking men are existing men. They are speaking of a new search for man, one that is not based upon a cosmic order which science has destroyed, one that is not rooted in the moral commitments of this or that culture group, one that is not firmly set in esoteric myths, but rather of one that is rooted in the free movement of the human spirit. It must be a search which begins and ends here. Whatever reality there is must be the reality which responds to the free, creative and personal spirit of man. His relation to reality, to himself, to other men, to God, must be authentically human and spiritual in this sense. The static, impersonal pictures and world-views of former times must go. The sun has set, at least temporarily, on the day of the picture people. Without accusation of betrayal or bitter repudiation of the past, without promise of permanence in the future, and with a deep sense of risk involved in revolution, we are witnessing a new dawn, the day of the drama people.

II. ALBUQUERQUE

Let the Dust Settle

At the Darwin Centennial Convention held at the University of Chicago in 1959, a gentleman by the name of Dr. Macdonald Critchley, a British neurologist and linguist, arose and reported on the evolution of man's capacity for language. In his researches, he had studied primate communities, especially the chimpanzees, and had this to say. In all his many years of research, he had never heard the chimp put two sounds together to make a sentence. The chimp makes twenty-one sounds and they all signify something. But he never puts two sounds together to make a sentence, to say that something is something. Man, he went on, is the only animal which speaks, which makes a language, and gives to existence a meaning over and above a passing reaction to a moment of pleasure or pain. Where there is an animal which puts two sounds together and makes a sentence, there you have a man.

I was impressed by this statement, and during a lecture in New York City soon after that I applied Critchley's analysis to the problem at hand—anthropological evidence for the uniqueness of man. Where you have an animal which puts two sounds together to make a sentence, there you have speech, and where you have speech, you have what the theologian calls spirit. Man is the only animal which puts two sounds together to make a sentence. . . .

One of the scientists present immediately raised his hand. "Do you have a zoo in Chicago?" he asked. "A good one," I replied, "Brookfield Zoo." "Ever visit it?" "Twice a year, religiously," I rejoined. "Well then," he went on in good humor, "if you were passing the chimpanzee cage and you overheard the chimp put two sounds together and make a sentence, what would you do?"

26

"I'd baptize him," I replied. Then, realizing that I had not em-
ployed the canon of sacramental discretion, I added, "Provided
he took instructions."

LECTURE AT THE UNIVERSITY OF NEW MEXICO, 1964
"ADAM AND ANTHROPOLOGY"

WITHOUT a doubt in my mind, it was the Sandia Lady, smiling down from the mountain crest, who changed my whole
life. Since that first morning when I awoke in Albuquerque
and threw open the blinds of my room looking out upon the
desert and the Sandia Mountains, I have never been the same.
I had come to rest and relax, to regain my health and energy,
and to finish *The Wisdom of Evolution*. It was February and
icy snows had covered the Midwest with interminable gloom.
Here the mountain air, the warm sun and unsullied skies
summoned forth my listless spirit. The ascetic brown and
orange of the desert sand, the rare scarlet blossoms on the
spiny cactus, the muted fragrance of early spring drew me out
into the open. In this incredibly splendid cradle of primitive
American man, Sandia, I regained my health and energy. But
most precious of all gifts, I discovered the spirit of man.

It must have been the laughter of the Lady of Sandia which
so renewed my spiritual life. The fossil men of North
America with whom my studies had made me acquainted
were the Folsom hunters of the Western plains and Sandia
man in New Mexico. One of the best known sites of Sandia
civilization was located just up the mountain side, a few miles
from my new home. I could see Sandia Crest from my writing desk, and for the first time in my evolutionary meditations, I began to tie up my personal existence with the

people who, now extinct, built their hearthside here, hunted and prayed here, lived and died here, over 20,000 years ago. It began to dawn on me that the evolution of *Homo sapiens* was *my* unfolding; that the hominid prehistory was *my* story. For the first time, I became aware of my spiritual continuity and solidarity with early mankind. They were no longer "those primitive creatures"; they were "my people."

The Sandia people were not just men on the hunt, tool-makers and fire builders. They were people who loved and hated, whose eyes gleamed with joy or burnt with tears of sadness. What about the women who watched their children at play and listened for strange noises of wild beasts? Was the birth of the child and his premature death in their arms merely the falling of a leaf from a tree? Or was the spirit of expectation, the joy of giving birth, the love of companion-ship and the planning for the future an intense response to their tenuous existence? What were their thoughts and aspirations as they watched the children, noisy with laughter as they played?

The thought began to lay hold of my mind. It was then that I became aware of the Lady up on Sandia Crest. As I walked in the afternoons along the mesa of the José Desert, the serpentine Rio Grande below me and the mountains in front of me, I imagined that I could see the Sandia woman standing with folded arms amidst the scraggy piñon trees, hair blowing in the wind, watching her child playing with the pine cones at her feet. Her laughter would ring out across the valley, startling the nervous finches and reminding the spinning cosmos that a conquering spirit possessed the land. For laughter is the infallible sign of the free human spirit reigning supreme over creation. No law of gravity can drag it down, no instinct can reach its heights, no oppression can crush it, no boundary can contain it. For by laughter, the spirit of man dwells with the gods.

How easy it is to drive a wedge between the sacred and the profane: to imagine that a man who must, perforce, be immersed in tilling the soil or hunting wild beasts, must thereby be crude and spiritually insensitive. "Primitive" is an academic term which captures none of the distinctive nuances of personal existence.

As Sandia man spent hours sewing together a mantle of mountain furs to clothe his wife, who is to say what span of those hours was labor and what was pure, joyous gift? And when she modeled that cloak for him, making every gesture to please his eyes and somehow return the gracious gift, were these moments of "primitive survival"? Or, were they rather moments during which she, standing in the radiant light of the early morning sun at the entrance of the cave, transformed his life with a touch of deepest love and understanding?

It was the almost daily communion with the Lady of the Mountain which opened up the past and projected the future of man for me. Once one's thoughts and imagination, one's loves and hopes, are allowed to course freely into the distant past and explore freely the distant future, even the present takes on a new and less illusory perspective. As the magnificent Cecropia moth emerges from its hard, grey-brown cocoon, stretches and sprawls until its dappled wings unfold in the warm New Mexico sun, so the clutter of little-mindedness and selfish anxiety fell away from my spirit as I walked under the gaze of the Lady of Sandia. She could not have known then that her son would create the twinkling colored lights of the motels and cafes along Menaul, and the terror of the atomic power at Los Alamos. She did not suspect that his play would range from giant jets to the miniature golf course, where daring wagers are made and sometimes paid. But she knew already the meaning of deep, personal, undying love which could be freely given, a gift which can never be expected, but which, once given, could re-create the face of the earth. And it was she who revealed this spiritual mystery to me. I am bound to her by a gift of love, and there is something in me from her that can never die. Whenever lack of imagination and creativity intrude upon my day, whenever meanness and pettiness and fretfulness threaten to throw up fences about my heart, I recall the generous, expansive warmth and laughter of the Lady of Sandia, and the way of my future again becomes clear.

* * * * * *

Much of the theologian's suspicion about the theory of evolution stems from a misplaced apprehension. He is afraid that science is robbing man of his spiritual uniqueness. He is afraid that if science convinces mankind that *Homo sapiens* arose from the great apes and is just a little more than an Australopithecine, the entire structure of human spirituality will collapse. This apprehension was once well-founded, in the times of Thomas Huxley and Herbert Spencer, who launched from Darwin's work devastating polemics at the

Christian idea of man. But much has happened in the last hundred years to change all that. The contemporary anthropologist knows little about the gross materialism of Huxley and Spencer, and cares less. To talk to him of these philosophies in the name of evolution would be as senseless as talking to an Italian Communist farmer about Marx and Lenin. To the latter, the Communist Party means simply the use of a tractor twice a year to plant and harvest his crops. To the evolutionist man of science today, the emergence of man from the primate world by a natural process of descent with modification by genetic mutation and natural selection is a highly documented explanation of a series of facts. For him, they bear little upon Christianity or philosophy or morals or any of the issues of past ages. He finds it difficult to understand why the Christian theologian is so reluctant to acknowledge the "fact of evolution."

Of course, to the world of fiction and popular science, which still feeds movies and television with a myopic and obsolete view of reality, the days of the Scopes Trial are still with us. When I mention that I, a priest, teach a course on the philosophy and theology of evolution, the average person expects that I am, of course, against the very thought of human emergence from the animal kingdom. Adam is close to the angels but not to the apes. What is rare, however, at least on the university campus, is the old "fundamentalist" opposition between scientific evolution and Christian teaching about the creation of man in the Bible. Occasionally, this "old-line" opposition is voiced, as it was in Albuquerque by one of the students attending my lecture. He indignantly disregarded the convergence of evidence for the natural origins of man and stated flatly: "As for me, I'll stand on the Bible any day!" But before any answer was required from the lecturer, another equally high-spirited student in what was probably a well-rehearsed improvisation stood up and retorted: "Why don't you stop standing on the Bible, pick it up, and read it intelligently!"

Most of the campus audience caught the important point of the chimpanzee anecdote. Science is affirming, not denying, the unicity of man. Anthropology is not constructed upon the maxim that man is just another anthropoid; quite the contrary, man is unique. Cultural anthropology has repudiated the old biologisims of the nineteenth century, and, in the main, regards biological evolution in man as a factor which is now superseded by a new principle of evolution, his psycho-social capacity. Man can never totally disengage himself from his biological and genetic determinants; they are the raw materials of his future. But man is the only animal that has the capacity to fashion his own future. No matter what the origins of this capacity, his destiny is shaped by his *freedom,* his *creativity,* and his *personality.* Man's progressive creation of speech, value systems and morality, art, science and technology, economy, community and society by freely and personally projecting his own future is the primary datum of contemporary anthropology, sociology and psychology. Science today affirms, not denies, the free, creative, personal uniqueness of *Homo sapiens,* and the philosopher or theologian who still sees evolution as an implicit denial of man's unqualified psychosocial superiority over the anthropoid world is fighting a battle of outworn cliché, not one of reality.

32

One of the university students raised an important question, however. Does the anthropologist, the scientist, see this superiority of man, his personal, creative freedom to fashion his future, as a *transcendent spiritual capacity* as do the philosopher and the theologian? This is a perceptive question. It is one thing to say that it is unintelligent to oppose science to religion, to oppose the prehistorian's account of origins to the biblical account, but quite another thing to say that their terms, their problems, their methods and their conclusions about reality are identical. The scientist does not speak of the *spirit* or *soul* of man; these are terms used by disciplines which approach reality from a point of view entirely different from that of empirical science. Even though the very capacity in man for personal, free creative design of his future is the sign and evidence to the theologian of the presence of an immanent transcendent spirit, the evolutionist limits himself to inferences which he can draw from the operational methods of his scientific investigation. That the operations of some of these materials may *further* imply transcendence, the existence of the *immaterial,* is something which science can neither affirm nor deny. The existence of the world of spirit and its relation to the world of matter is a perennial preoccupation of the deepest thought of man. The advances of scientific thought have cleared away many pseudo-problems and have eliminated many old-wives' tales and misconceptions about the world of matter. But contemporary science has by no means removed the problem of the spirit of man. Science does not use the concept "spirit"; nor does it deny the validity of the concept. The existence of the transcendent reality is a concern which belongs, rather, to the humanities, philosophy and theology.

This answer was not wholly satisfactory, and a number of questions followed in swift succession. What has happened in the last few years to change the attitudes in this science-religion question? Are all scientists and theologians in agreement with my attempt to bring about a harmonious interdisciplinary statement about evolutionary origins? Do theologians and philosophers know enough about scientific origins to have a right to sit in on such a discussion? Do scientists accept theology and philosophy as valid disciplines with their own authentic subject and method? Were there no real unsolved problems in the area of evolutionary origins which still brings science and the Bible into open confrontation? Was not this concordance of approach which I was suggesting only a pseudo-resolution?

The discussion was allowed to go on for an hour or more, and bit by bit the issues became clearer. Unquestionably, the advances in professional evolutionary science of prehistory, genetics, ecology and physical anthropology have made the inferences of evolutionary theory more sure, its methods more rigorous and better documented, and its conclusions more available to the educated public. Since 1940, the remarkable strides taken in biblical studies have made it abundantly clear that the Bible is a religious and moral revelation, not a manual of scientific origins. Much of the philosophical dust has settled about the relations of order and chance in an evolutionary universe. Professional competence has cut away most of the opposition among the disciplines by the simple process of better understanding.

34

But there is still great failure of professional competence, both on the part of the scientist and the theologian. These problems require a specialized knowledge on several levels which only a few men have had the opportunity to acquire. The theologian has by no means proved that he has a truly professional intellectual contribution to make to mutual problems concerning man's origin and destiny. He has not manifested an openmindedness and awareness of how much he needs the assistance of scientific disciplines in his own work of theology. How a theologian can think and teach and write about creation, about the nature of man, and about the relationship between man and God without a competence in cosmology, psychology, sociology and comparative religion, is beyond the comprehension of contemporary enlightenment. And with good reason: it simply cannot be done. On the other hand, the scientist is not always so careful about neutrality in areas of moral value and religious affirmation. But, on the whole, the second half of the twentieth century has opened with a remarkable respect among professional scientists, philosophers and theologians for each other's efforts in disentangling and resolving the problem of human origins, a respect which promises, theoretically at least, that the old war between religion and science will no longer be waged on the university campus.

There are deep, unsolved problems in the area of evolutionary origins which still threaten to bring scientific prehistory and some forms of Christianity into open confrontation. One such question is whether man arose on the planet as an individual (monogenism) or as a member of a population (polygenism). Evolutionary science regards polygenism as the most probable condition of human origins simply because evolutionary theory never does (nor can it) concern itself with individuals, whether they be camels, tree-sparrows or humans. Monogenism is, to the scientist, theoretically improbable; he does not consider it an acceptable explanation of origins of any animal species. On the other hand, many Catholic theologians consider the teaching of Christianity on the origins of original sin to be incompatible with any form of polygenism.

Science studies the origins of man; theology studies the origin of moral fault, especially as it is treated by the traditional understanding of biblical revelation in *Genesis,* the Wisdom books and the Pauline letters. In 1950, Pope Pius XII expressed what seemed then to be an impasse between evolutionary science and Christian teaching in his encyclical *Humani generis.* In this document, polygenism was not condemned as formally contrary to orthodox Christian teaching, but was ruled untenable because of what appeared to be insurmountable difficulties. However, as one might expect, much research has accumulated between that date and the present, and there are a good number of responsible theologians and Scripture scholars who are proposing ways of resolving the difficulties posed in *Humani generis.* It is apparent that evolutionary theory is neutral about the matter of the origin of moral fault, important though this is in unraveling the problem of the meaning of human existence. It may soon be equally apparent that the moral theologian's quest for the source of the presence of moral evil in man's life may also be neutral about the physical origins of *Homo sapiens.* It would be an oversimplification to say that scientific human evolution raises no problems for the Christian philosopher and theologian. But today there is professional competence and respect among the disciplines involved which never before obtained. The prospects for resolution of common issues are now very promising.

I returned to my room late that night. Albuquerque was asleep and I was glad to be alone again with only a small travel-clock ticking away the last hour of the day. Speaking the night through with a serious audience of university students and faculty was a tremendous strain. I used to travel with the University of Michigan gymnastic squad which performed for hours under the lights in gymnasiums about the country, but it was nothing like this. When the meet was over, we rallied round a steak, and, in the noise of jolly nonsense, we forgot the matter in minutes. All that was left after an evening on the horizontal bar or the flying rings was a sore muscle and a new callus. But lecturing was a different kind of "performance." When you speak, you leave something of yourself back in the auditorium; you remain somehow among those young men and women. And they remain with you. For they also spoke, revealing something of reality through their words, which were alive, responding to your words, which were alive.

* * * * * *

I set my alarm. In less than twelve hours, I'd be back in Chicago. But the lecture continued within me. There was something that had been added to my being, something which I had brought away with me. I was uneasy about something. Was it a word that had been spoken? A question unanswered, or poorly answered? There are always these. No, it was something which had not been said. It was something about my own attitude which this discussion revealed to me. There was a dimension to this problem of communication between evolutionary science and religion which was escaping me. Deep down, I knew that I had been superficial, that theoretical concordance and harmony among the disciplines was only one dimension, perhaps not even the most important. As one of the students had said: "If it is so simple, so easy, why do the theologians and the scientists stay so far apart ... ?"

That was the crux. The scientist and the philosopher and the theologian are now speaking to each other about a common problem; they see the prospects of interdisciplinary resolution of some of them. But what makes us so sure that the discussion will not break down—that anything will come of it? Is it not that we still retain the language, the speech of opposition, even though we expect to find harmony? We have begun to communicate, but we are still using the expressions of old opposition. We are refusing to let the dust settle!

It has taken one hundred years of tedious research and discipline to mend the breakdown of communication between the world of evolutionary views of Darwin, Spencer and Huxley, and the world of Christian thought. But the distance between theoretical communication of common issues and the free, personal creative expression about these realities is still very great. There is a deep, basic, unconscious impediment to human understanding and sympathy in these matters

38

which stems, not from the issues themselves, but from the cultural traditions in which man's speaking and thinking are formed. Scientists, philosophers and theologians are professional, and they are carefully raised in a tradition canonized by their trade. None of them is wholly *free,* for each must think and feel and act from within the walls of his tradition. The *creative* scientist, philosopher or theologian is rare, for tradition generates a condition in which the *status quo* is always preferred. Most scientists, philosophers and theologians are hopelessly *impersonal,* and they place a premium upon communicating their disciplines in the appropriate language without expressing themselves personally. To be free, creative and personal in these professional areas would seem to be an infidelity to the cause they represent.

Why this insistence upon impartiality of viewpoint? Because the point of view, the picture of reality, not the drama of interpersonal life, is preferred. Deep down, the audience was reacting to the problem of human origins from the drama of their own lives, the human value and meaning which follows from our insights. Yet the discussion among the professionals remains, by definition and perforce, in the order of a construct, a world-picture, a vision of reality. The basic oppositions were only superficially on the level of reality; they were fundamentally caused by a clash of world-pictures. The theologian, the philosopher and the scientist each had his own into which the realities discussed must fit. The drama of life, where speaking really takes place, must wait. Picture people were still calling the shots. Who but the Sandia Lady, with her tears and her smiles at the sight of her family from the mountain crest, illumined for me the drama of life with this light of freedom and creative love? The dust would one day really settle, and men would break the professional barriers to true spiritual solidarity. As the musical sound of her laughter echoed down the mountain side I rejoiced—and slept soundly.

III. CHAPEL HILL

Flying the Flag

It is folly to think that evolutionary unfolding in time and space applies less to the spirit of man than to his body. There is every evidence that man's morals and manners have evolved as completely as his anatomy. There is now good reason to believe that man's biological evolution was not the cause but the result of his psychosocial evolution. But to say this is not to say that human value is a mere projection of animal emotion, nor that in the most primitive of men, there are but diluted traces of stable moral rules of individual and social life.

Cannibalism is often regarded, at least in the popular imagination, as a primitive state of human existence. Indeed, some very early groups manifested forms of human flesh-eating. But it is a mistake to think that they had no morals, that they were incapable or unaware of the laws of justice. They were a just people, with high, almost puritanical, moral sanctions.

"Why, then," you might ask a cannibal, "do you eat men?" He would reply that, as a matter of fact, those who know cannibals know that they do not eat men—they can be disposed of on the spot for taking a man's life. "But," you might complain to our cannibal friend, "I just saw you put one in the pot!" "That was not a man," he would reply, wagging his head. "What, then, is a man?" you would anxiously ask, aware that the answer to this question is of paramount importance. "A member of the tribe. . . ."

Lecture at the University of North Carolina, 1964
"The Evolution of Morals"

It had happened again. Now, more than ever before, I am convinced that motivation, inspiration and creativity are, in great part, a function of the environment in which a man finds himself. Flying from Chicago to Raleigh in a cloudless sky, 33,000 feet high at 625 miles an hour, crossing rivers and mountains, leaping from city to city, reshuffles all the images and ideas, and one can sit down to write any hour of the day. It is not simply the romantic feeling of seeing new sights, meeting new people—the sense of space and time unfolding —I am deeply and personally touched by new conditions of existence. I come alive.

Lecturing in Chicago had been a real workout, a tiring ordeal, but not very stimulating. Not because the people were themselves less interesting and generous, but because it was my "home town." Associations in that city have jelled and emotions have become structured by memories of long con-straint, a necessary condition of human existence in which there is a job to be done day after day after day. Just as soon as I reclined in the Boeing 707 to Charlotte, North Carolina, I lost all the hardening of my mental and emotional arteries. At first, I was reluctant to lose this sense of freedom by talk-ing to anyone. Even the pleasant Hawaiian woman and her two-year-old daughter sitting next to me offered no fascina-tion. But as the Blue Ridges appeared ahead and the sun bronzed the rusty soil of Kentucky and Carolina, I began to feel the urgency of existence again. The materials of creativity were again in my power.

The Chapel Hill campus is without doubt one of the most beautiful I have ever visited. Mockingbirds and wood thrushes dart about in the afternoon shadows. A strong sweet aroma of over-blossomed flowers pervades the air. No one is in a hurry, yet there is the preoccupation and high seriousness you expect from the university student. The feeling I had on this spring afternoon was that I did not belong here. I was an alien, very respected in my clerical collar, but a visitor. On my part, I had none of the spiritual constraints of promoting a cause. I was not a salesman representing a client. I had been invited to address this body of students on the subject of the evolution of morals, a subject with momentous consequences upon our culture, but today I was not speaking as a member of a fraternity, representing a "point of view."

Perhaps the most important feature about these past three weeks had been the intellectual mobility which travelling and lecturing afforded me. I was now far enough from my base, my home, my place of work, my institute of affiliation, my family, to feel almost no emotional tie with what they think or do. I did not love or admire those back there less, yet the organized community work, imperceptibly and quite naturally, had defined the limits of my intellectual vision for years. One cannot easily disengage himself from his beginnings, his roots, his affiliations—yet on Chapel Hill, on the eve of this lecture, those emotional ties seemed weightless and far away. A new thing was at work within me, a spiritual economy which alerted me to the cultural baggage I was carrying about with me.

We had dinner in one of the halls on campus. A small contingent of officers from the Newman Center escorted me and provided information and insights into the charm of Chapel Hill. But in spite of the enthusiasm and alertness of the gracious hosts of the dinner, the conversation soon became

43

stuffy; at least, so it seemed to *me*. I suppose it may have been my fault. For all they knew, I wanted nothing better than to talk about my professional preoccupations; philosophy of science, evolution, polygenism, natural law. So the discussion went on, quite insistently, about these matters. Would they have been crushed to know what my mood really called for? A few feet away was a juke box and I would have given anything to have heard Dean Martin's "Everybody Loves Somebody Sometime" or Nat King Cole's "That Sunday, That Summer"! But I had only arrived among my new friends, and I could not presume to threaten the image of the intellectual so quickly. You can take your shoes off only in your own home. As I sat there listening to the difficulties which changes in the Church's attitudes have raised among the young intellectuals, my mind slipped back to Biloxi, Mississippi, where I was walking on the beach just a few bright mornings ago.

*　　*　　*　　*　　*　　*

The black-capped terns were swirling, knifing their way across the salty Gulf waters a few feet above me. The feel of sand slipping underfoot reminded me of my childhood on Lake Erie when I searched out that same fascinating bird with my binoculars. But this time the tern was not a bird to be identified; it was a mood, striking out against constraint. The lapping water reflected their frolicking as they called out "A-dell," "A-dell," and liberated themselves from the downpress of the wind. The warm Mississippi sun dissolved all my anxieties, and I could follow the terns' flight without

44

thought, without locating responsibility. They were birds, to be sure, and they had to feed, to nest, to fly, to die. But they were improvising with a swift, sudden change of pace. At any moment, they might dive into the water for a shimmering silver morsel of sea-food. At any moment, they might disappear into a cloud and never be seen again. But they were "playing it by ear," free from the pattern of organized constraint.

Then that night there was dinner at the Friendship House on Biloxi Bay with an old seminary friend. We had stuffed flounder, chablis, parfait praline. When we left the restaurant the April evening was lovely under a blanket of unfamiliar constellations. As we drove along Frazie Bay on the Gulf, the sands were dotted with the light of open fires. "What are the fires?" I asked. "Oh, it's a familiar sight in the spring and the fall. The students and the tourists swim during the day along the beach and then when it turns cool and the sun sets, they light fires and cook their meals." "Every night it is like this?" I asked. "Oh, yes," he replied, "but God only knows what goes on." "Why?" I asked. "It's a beautiful night and I'd like to be with friends around an open fire on the beach myself." "Well," he sighed, "knowing human nature to be what it is, no good can come of it."

I was suddenly miffed. Not that his remark was unexpected. I had heard such moralizing before; custodians of religion are often practicing such dire predictions about the human race. Nor was I under any illusions about student life, especially on April evenings along the warm Gulf coast. Perhaps it was the black-capped terns cavorting in the morning sun which set me off. It was that phrase "knowing human nature to be what it is . . ." Just what does "knowing human nature" consist of, besides a handful of old wives tales? And just what does "knowing human nature" say about those people out there enjoying the open fires? Not a thing. There is only one way to find out and that is to share the open fire with the persons on the beach, to *speak with them,* which is to live with them. It is the distance between the ponderousness of the phrase, so acceptable to some cultures as a sign of wisdom, and the emptiness of the idea that disturbed me. How often does one hear that neat inventory of perceptive definitions: "Protestant religion is irrational"; "Scientists are materialists"; "Hollywood stars are irresponsible"; "Jews are money mad"; "Baptists are bigots"; "Negroes are unfit for society"; "Catholics are hypocrites." It is so easy to cultivate a tribal mentality. All you need is the right dialect, the language of typological thought where taxonomy is simple and judgment is swift. There is but one shortcoming with this language: there is no communication with others outside the tribe.

* * * * * *

The Chapel Hill crowd was easily touched off and was ready to do battle over some of the issues if necessary. I am a firm believer that an audience catches the speaker's mood, his intellectual and emotional temper, like an infection. I spoke for an hour on the evolution of human morals, supporting the proposition that human moral law has unfolded in space and time, bit by bit, just as man's genetic capacities have evolved. And that further, if you insist that the human spirit is immune to the influences of evolutionary changes even now going on in the cosmos, you are "angelizing" man into an illusion and a caricature of reality. This is not an easy subject to deal with because you have to balance two terms which have always caused confusion: *matter* and *spirit*. The trouble broke out when I attempted to describe, as best I could in this context, the disparate origins of the human body and the human spirit, without shattering the unity of the human personality. How, without it having a jarring effect, do you express the fact that the spirit of man emerged simultaneously with the evolution of the human body, but not *out of* cosmic matter and energy? That God *specially* created the human spirit without upsetting the natural unfolding of the material creation? The only way I can handle the matter is to take it in fragments; I have to use more than one set of terms and, in the end, I have to resort to putting the pieces together like a toy puzzle. It doesn't come out very neatly.

A small pocket of rather agitated students in one corner of the auditorium demanded clarification of this point, and for almost a half hour we struggled with the matter-spirit-evolution problem. The general peacefulness of Chapel Hill was temporarily marred by this prolonged and heated discussion. Finally, one of the discussants, a graduate genetics student, called a rather abrupt halt to this interchange with these words: "Well, sir, you seem to be in the unenviable position of having to affirm the evolution of the whole man on the one hand because science demands it, and having to affirm the transcendence (and therefore non-evolution) of the soul just because your Church tells you to. We scientists do not have to play such games; we just affirm evolution and deny the soul. It's simple and honest that way."

I took the occasion to thank him for his honesty, and especially for his simplicity—which everyone seemed to enjoy—and on that pleasant note we adjourned for the evening. But the young geneticist sensed that his remark to me was a rather "low blow," and he cordially invited me and a few others to pursue this matter further in his fraternity lounge. We all agreed upon this sensible suggestion. The jovial, gentle Chapel Hill atmosphere pervaded the discussion, and much more was accomplished during these moments than during the earlier part of the evening.

In the back of my mind was surely the capricious free flight of the terns over the Biloxi Bay, and the night fires on the beach. Where had I heard that said before? "You have to affirm the soul because your Church tells you to." Was it so different from "knowing human nature . . ."? There are two very effective ways to end a discussion, and, in short order, the young geneticist had employed them both: *flying the flag* and the *falling inflection*. They go together like twin brothers. Either of them is rhetorically conclusive because each brings about the collapse of communication. There is nothing left to be said.

The falling inflection is easy to detect, easy to understand, and easy to employ. All one has to do is put a period at the end of one's sentence. It is the emotion of finality; the last word has been spoken. This rhetorical quality is usually found in all those who are accustomed, both professionally and privately, to decide matters, to settle issues. If a ruler employs this falling inflection, he is called a tyrant; if a housewife employs it, she is called a shrew. But not uncommonly, the falling inflection parades in the name of virtue, and it is called candor, forthrightness, clarity, decisiveness, lucidity. Whatever it is called and wherever it is found, the falling inflection puts an end to the matter, and when the matter is debate, discussion, dialogue, then it has no place at all.

Because of their leadership image, there are three professional groups especially addicted to the use of the falling inflection: scientists, philosophers and theologians. The reason is clear: They are all traditions which are necessarily constructed upon canons of judgment, rules of procedure, method. They are ever called upon to make definite, rather decisive, statements. The requirements of the culture demand that science, philosophy and theology provide summaries, manuals, textbooks, compendiums. The temptation is to canonize too much, to use the falling inflection, to close the issue. In matters of research and interdisciplinary discussion, such as the question of the relation of matter and spirit, impatience in the name of decision can too readily put a period at the end of the sentence. The effect is lethal.

The genial group recognized this rhetorical folly at once, and the geneticist apologized for his precipitous manner at the lecture. But why, he asked, did I object to his statement, "We scientists do not have to play such games; we just affirm evolution and deny the soul"? It was a statement of fact with great logical economy, he thought. And, of course, the statement has a razor-like precision. The only difficulty is that it moves the discussion over into a restricted zone. It is hoisting the flag of science, and, in effect, demanding that the language, the method, the rules, the entire communication be adjusted to the superior vision or view of things, in this case the "scientific view." It is the tribal mentality all over again; authentic communication ceases when you force the man with whom you are speaking to translate everything into your dialect. A world-view may be represented in this way, but the interpersonal drama of speech and discussion is impossible. Aside from whether the geneticist's statement was valid or not, it is begging the question to say that the point of view of the family tradition is superior, and that all would be well if everyone would rally round the same family flag.

There is a paradox here. The advancement of every great movement, every great cause, has required the organization of teams, schools, unions, fraternities, parties. These, in turn, require "party lines," mottoes, "battle cries," family escutcheons, team colors and songs which encourage fidelity to one's own. Internal motivation to carry forward a team work demands a kind of family pride which is built upon the excellence of a tradition and a point of view. In spite of the "objectivity" of science and the detachment of the "scientific method," the meetings of scientific organizations are marked by family commitments and clannish vocabulary. In evolutionary circles, one is a "Darwinist," or a "Lamarckian," or a "synthesist." For the interpretation of the fossil record, the view of Simpson is opposed to the view of Schindewolf; in genetics it is the micromutationism of Dobzhansky versus the macromutationism of Goldschmidt. And so it goes. No one would take exception to "school fidelity," for the growth of scientific theory demands adherents and articulate representatives who show up at conventions if for no other reason than to explain and defend a position. The internal value of flying the family flag to the progress of team work is great. But when it is no longer a matter of the family, the clan and the tribe, but a matter of the university, the nation, the community at large, the family flag must be pulled down.

The same must be said of theological matters. To the Christian, there is no more valuable and sacred an entrance into the reality of human happiness than the revelation of the Incarnation of Christ, but this revelation can be made known and embraced only in open discussion and liberty of conscience. Christ's command "Go and teach all nations" generates an obligation, not to form a narrow family mentality of fidelity to one's own, but of necessity to learn the language of free discussion. Vatican Council II has reaffirmed this basic freedom of conscience, and its corollary is, it seems to me, pulling down the family flag. Such an apostolate of free discussion, far from cultivating an insipid compromise of thought and belief, demands even deeper, clearer and stronger faith.

The students who had now gathered at the lounge were still wondering what I had to say about the remark, "your Church tells you to . . ." This was the implication of the whole criticism of my stand, in short, that I was flying the flag of the Catholic Church and that was why I had to take such a complicated stand. Now I faced the matter squarely in my own mind, perhaps for the first time. In the last hundred years of controversy between science and religion on the question of evolution, it had not been the scientist who was most addicted to the flying of the flag. It was the philosopher and the theologian. In my few years of experience, discussing this question of evolution among many professional groups, without question the philosopher and the theologian found it the more difficult to disengage themselves from family ties.

One might object to this judgment. Scientists are no less inclined to ideological commitments, it might be asserted, for almost all well-known scientists—Newton, Einstein, Planck, Darwin, Mach, to mention a handful—elaborated their thought from within the orientation of a world-view. Einstein, for example, did not fully "believe in" indeterministic quantum physics because, as he said, "I cannot believe that God plays dice with the universe." But in light of the history of evolutionary thought, I think that it is true to say that the flag-raisers were largely the philosophers and theologians, not the scientists. The reason is that the philosopher and theologian are more explicitly involved in matters of human values. The scientist *may* have deep commitments concerning moral and religious values, and *may* utilize his scientific researches to promote an ideology. A good example of this today is the writing of Sir Julian Huxley, who teaches the religion of evolutionary humanism. But this is not expected of the scientists, whereas it is expected of theologians and philosophers. They are expected to discover, to propose and to promote a world-view and an ideology of human happiness.

It is a fact which must be acknowledged, that most philosophers and theologians are brought up as apprentices to a religious point of view, and that much of their work is directly or indirectly apostolic and ideological. They have an axe to grind, and that is to bring about a change in society by means of their world-view. I have seen it over and over again. Whether the man is a Thomist or a Teilhardian, the capacity for discussion of contemporary scientific issues is highly circumscribed by the demands of his commitments. The young geneticist's question, "Are you saying that man has a spirit because you really think so, or because your Church tells you so?" is a valid question, but one which appears embarrassing and unfair to a "family man." From my own experience I can number on one hand the philosophers and theologians I know who are really concerned about the factual evidence for evolution. They are preoccupied with ideas and theories about human value and meaning, largely drawn from a tradition which is very much a family one. They go to the university, the community, the discussion-at-large, with a message to be delivered, an apostolate to accomplish, and a world-view to promote—not a discussion-drama to be entered into. It is true that we cannot exist without ideologies and religious convictions, without prophets and conversions. It is equally clear, however, that it takes a great deal more than a religious message and a benevolent motive to set into motion an authentic discussion in the intellectual community.

Is my problem with the matter-spirit difficulty in evolutionary discussion, then, complicated merely because I am under some ideological pressure? Do I have a difficulty in accounting for the emergence of the human spirit solely because "my Church" insists upon the special creation of the soul by God? No, for this is an oversimplified diagnosis. Philosophy has battled the question of the relation between the human spirit and the material universe since its beginnings. Theology of whatever orientation, Christian, Jewish, Eastern, has attempted to plumb the mystery of the human spirit, and would find the geneticist's simple denial of the existence of a problem very naïve. For that matter, a random sampling of articles in recent issues of the British neurological journal *Brain,* for example, would reveal that to scientists like Sherrington, Penfield, Brain and Eccles the mind-body problem remains one of the perennial and most vexing issues that confronts the scientific as well as the philosophic world today.

But it must be admitted that the Catholic tradition of philosophy and theology in which I was raised, the intellectual family in which I grew up, provides an approach which insists, perhaps far too much, that the discussion follow certain lines which may make the evolutionary issue unduly complicated. The Catholic philosophical and theological tradition, at least until recently, accented a kind of dualism which does not easily fit the evolutionary unfolding. Father Teilhard de Chardin has suggested a monistic approach which may be of assistance in unraveling this dialogical issue. But the matter-spirit problem is a *real* one, one which neither science nor philosophy has adequately probed in terms of each others' methods and insights. It is by no means a mere ideological question as it appeared to be to the young geneticist.

We had to leave the issue there. Was there really any hope for dialogue between science and religion, discussion unhampered by the falling inflection and flying the flag? Was it realistic to expect that the scientist, the philosopher and the theologian could put aside their family predilections for the sake of the community? No one was in the mood to open this issue, for time was running out. As we parted, we seemed of a mind, however, that there is a grave responsibility in human discussion, whether public or private, to desist from riding herd on the spirit, to haul down the flag if possible, and to avoid the falling inflection at all costs. Peace had once more descended upon lovely Chapel Hill, and I went home.

*   *   *   *   *   *

On my way back to Chicago and my classes at the Aquinas Institute, I took the opportunity to visit my family home in Monroe, Michigan. While there, I spent one sunny afternoon visiting my father and step-mother. We were sitting, chatting, and I was sipping a can of beer. Suddenly, a great din arose across the way, and the sound of hilarious laughter and a partial chorus of "Ida, Sweet as Apple Cider" broke the calm of our conversation. "What in heaven's name is that?" exclaimed my father. "Oh, they're drinking beer again," my step-mother said, slightly upset. "But *he's* drinking beer," said my father, amusingly pointing my way. Her quick reply was, "You know that's different." I smiled as I finished my Bud, admiring the dear woman for her instinctive family fidelity.

IV. STANFORD

The Folly of the Package Deal

Extinction of man, failure creatively and freely to adapt, can come from blindly following in the path of either traditional or contemporary intuitions, from following uncritically either Aquinas or Sartre. Failure to orientate man's world-view in space and time, to see how epigenic unfolding enters into all that man is and does, will result in illusion. Total immersion in the timely without discovering the supratemporal meaning of existence, and without spiritual openness to the Divine, will just as surely threaten man's ability to survive. It is not simply a question of updating Aquinas or providing bibliographies of Sartre. Polemics which barter a word from Sartre for a word from Aquinas are futile, and they make spiritual solidarity based upon authentic insight doubly difficult.

Yet there is great expectation. Man must look to the future of Homo sapiens. *It is no longer simply a question of the Greek Academy or Lyceum, of a Scholastic synthesis, of cultivating manners, of technological prowess, or even a liberal education. It is a question of survival by creative, free, spiritual solidarity. The solution is to call forth every authentic insight into harmonious bearing upon the issue: to fashion the future of man. We cannot afford to lose a single insight into reality whether traditional or contemporary. Neither Aquinas nor Sartre suffices. With the best of both, we stand a chance of survival.*

LECTURE AT STANFORD UNIVERSITY, 1965
"SARTRE, AQUINAS AND THE LEMMINGS"

It was not difficult to understand why I arrived a half day early on the Stanford campus. February in Chicago is almost intolerable. The grim, bitter-cold, endless hours of winter wear on, and by February not an ounce of optimistic energy is left. Each year I find it harder to last until the warm April rains.

I deposited my baggage in my temporary quarters and began to explore the vast expanse of the Stanford mall. The warm sun and the deep green of the grass captivated me. Before long I was standing in front of an enormous campus bulletin board upon which, among other things, announcements of lectures and other activities appeared. What an unbelievable plethora of extracurricular events, literally scores of seminars, lectures, field trips, athletic meets, professional discussions and cultural programs! So it is at every school where tens of thousands of students gather for their professional training, and one has to marvel at this opportunity for endless enrichment offered on campuses like Harvard, Michigan, Berkeley and U.C.L.A. I remembered how difficult it was to organize my day at the University of Michigan with hundreds of opportunities like this before me.

Sure enough, there, abandoned in the midst of all those fine opportunities, was the announcement of my lecture: "'Evolution and the Future of Man' by Dr. Raymond J. Nogar, author of *The Wisdom of Evolution*." I had to smile. On the campus of private schools, the lecturer was always given the assembly hall or the auditorium; here at Stanford, I was to be heard in one of a score of lecture rooms, number 208. Of the thousands of students and faculty members on campus, only those would attend who saw this announcement and were interested in the subject—and had some free time. But this was a blessing: my audience would not be large; neither would it be a captive one.

Whether it was the leisurely splendor of the California skies or my own intellectual mood, I did something which is dangerous for a lecturer to do. I decided to change my address at the last moment. I had done this once before, at the University of Wichita. The situation was similar: a small, informal, professional group of scientists, philosophers and theologians responding to a topic which was not specialized. I had, of course, given them the option of hearing the original talk or of discussing a chapter of my forthcoming book, a discussion which would be of great value to me. They were quite willing to make the change. I would do the same thing here; I would ask them to discuss an article I was in the process of writing—one called "Sartre, Aquinas and the Lemmings," a problem directly related to the subject of evolution and the future of man, yet more philosophical (since it involved Sartre and Aquinas) than the original lecture.

Again, I was very happy that I made the last-minute switch, for the Stanford group was exceptionally cordial and in a reflective mood. The prospects of discussing an article about to be published promised an informality which a canned address lacks. The discussion which followed, lasting far longer than the appointed time, confirmed my instinct that given a personal, intellectual challenge, the thoughtful man readily abandons the workaday world to ponder the mystery of "the way things are." From that discussion on the Stanford campus I received an invaluable insight. One of the most serious threats to interdisciplinary discussion, whether on evolution or any other subject, is: *the folly of the package deal.*

No matter what the aspect of the evolutionary question, the scientist comes to the discussion with a different contribution from that of the philosopher and the theologian. The scientist, by temperament and training, deals in *fragments;* the philosopher and theologian, in their concern for a world-view, tend rather to deal in *systems.* This comparison must not be pressed too far, for the scientist, too, has his "world" in which his research finds orientation. But the contrast is valid to a measure. The scientist isolates a tiny sector of reality and explores its materials, its activity under highly controlled conditions. He wants to know *how* it operates. The philosopher is looking for meaning, value, the *why* of, not a tiny sector of the cosmos, but the entirety of existence. The cosmologist asks: At the present hypothetical rate of the expanding universe, how old are the most distant galaxies? The philosopher looks at the same universe and asks: Why not nothing? The first kind of question necessarily involves a fragment of existence; the second kind of question tends, rather, to the systematic involvement of many areas of experience.

There is another reason for this contrast. Scientists are brought up in an apprenticeship of research and problem solving. Most philosophers and theologians are brought up in an apprenticeship of pedagogy, of teaching a tradition. Of course, there are exceptions: many scientists never do much research and are preoccupied with teaching and writing text-books; some rare philosophers and theologians spend their lives in specialized research, solving problems. But even on the pedagogical side of both professions, the scientist is more likely to be specialized. Philosophers and theologians are often asked to teach many broad areas of thought: logic, epistemology, history of philosophy, metaphysics, ethics. Their subjects, their method, their traditions incline them to become "package dealers."

A very good example of the kind of thing I am talking about is the recent problem in moral theology which has arisen in the area of family regulation and contraceptive birth control. There is a very acute "problem" for ethical philosophy and moral theology. Not too many scientists would recognize immediately any similarity between this kind of "problem" and their research problem, simply because they do not often see a philosopher or theologian approach matters like these with an exact method and scientific detachment. The reason for this is that not very many philosophers and theologians have the training, the background, the time, the energy, the professional competence to assume the responsibility of this issue *as a problem*. Too many discussions have to do, not with problem solving, but with the clichés of the trade, defending either a conservative or a liberal system or attitude. The issue is examined in terms of the consequences to system, rather than on the level of independent and detached research. This is an ideological attitude, not a philosophical one, and when the philosopher or theologian is thus oriented in his thought his contribution is more often than not a "package deal."

This statement requires explanation. In itself, there is nothing wrong with presenting a systematic view of any problem. By "package deal" I mean the insistence that if

60

you buy a part, you must buy the whole; if you sell a part, you must sell the whole of the product. A few examples will make this clear. For almost one hundred years, evolution was opposed by philosophical and religious groups because they thought, erroneously, that materialism, even atheism, necessarily were part of the package deal of evolution. In his encyclical *Pacem in Terris,* Pope John XXIII warned against associating contemporary Communism with old Marxists teachings, condemning out of hand any recent developments. Much of the work of Sigmund Freud has been rejected in the past because of the ideology which was thought to go with the psychological insights as part of the package. The mechanical, mathematical and behavioristic models used in psychology, anthropology and sociology have increased our knowledge about *Homo sapiens* enormously. This fact by no means implies that a materialistic, mechanistic or behavioristic philosophy of man must be accepted. Men who tend to think in terms of systems, tend to reject out of hand the valuable insights which emerge from other patterns of thought, largely because they are committed to "package-deal" thinking.

Package-deal thinking is also evident on the selling side of the product. Many thinkers who have been brought up in a systematic tradition of thought are unsatisfied if they merely contribute an insight into a problem: they insist on selling the whole system or nothing. At a distance, we see the folly of this package deal immediately. One of the egregious mistakes the Communists in Russia made was to insist that if one accepts the communistic theory of economics, he must also accept Lysenko's theory of genetics. The weakness of this ideological thinking became evident when Lysenko's theory of genetics was repudiated by the world of science, but not without bringing into further disrepute the ideology which would exercise such systematic control. No one disputes the validity of many of the basic socio-economic theories of Marx and Hegel. The doctrine of social determinism is axiomatic in the scientific research of modern sociology. Here is an insight of great value. But to insist upon a communistic theory of man, of metaphysics, of law, of ethics, of international politics, of science, art and religion is destructive of this valid insight.

Because of the devastating effect of certain wholesale ideologies, especially those sanctioned by the authority of a powerful organization or even a culture, contemporary Western thought has been scrupulously critical of any philosophy or theology which bears this stamp of systematic ideology. Because of its acceptance by Catholic culture of past ages and its diversity of development into every branch of human knowledge and action, one of the most criticized philosophical systems in Europe and America is Thomism. The chief criticism has been leveled at the insistence of many of its adherents that if you accept a part of Thomism, you must accept the whole: its cosmology, its psychology, its metaphysics, its logic, its theology, its attitude towards Christian spirituality. As a consequence, Thomism has fallen upon evil days, not because its basic insights are invalid, but because many areas of its system are no longer acceptable.

Thomism is not alone in this condemnation. The systems of Descartes, Comte, Hegel, Kant, Bergson and Whitehead (to mention a few) have received like treatment by contemporary thinkers. But the fate of Thomism is doubly dramatic because it is undergoing the radical criticism in America today that it underwent in Europe from 1920–1950. If one carefully examines the writings of the main European thinkers of the last fifty years, he will see at once that they were trying to fight free of the assumptions, whether religious, philosophical or theological, of systems imposed upon the mind by powerful organizations or by the culture itself. Kierkegaard, Heidegger, the later Husserl, Merleau-Ponty, Scheler, Sartre pointed their phenomenological fingers in accusation at the illusions of established philosophical and theological systems like Thomism. Logical atomism, logical positivism, linguistic and conceptual analysis, so different from the phenomenologists in many details, joined them in this devastating condemnation. By 1940, Thomism as a system was dead in Europe.

But if Thomism as a system was dead, Thomism as a priceless fountain of realistic insights was more alive than ever. If men like Jacques Maritain and Reginald Garrigou-Lagrange failed to promote Thomistic logic, metaphysics, aesthetics, natural philosophy and theology as a single system, the insights of Thomas Aquinas were not lost in the fragmentary contributions of Karl Rahner, Yves Congar, Edouard Schillebeeckx and Josef Pieper. No serious thinker will deny a single realistic contribution to the resolution of a problem which is harassing the human spirit. It makes little difference if that contribution originates from a tradition which is Kantian, Hegelian, Aristotelian or Cartesian. If the dualism of matter-form can be presented in such a way as to resolve a problem in contemporary physics, as Werner Heisenberg suggests that it might, then let it be put forward. If Karl Rahner is correct in saying that natural-law orientation can be combined with existential personalism to develop a realistic morality which will help solve the birth-control dilemma, then it ought to be attempted. If the stability of the order of nature in Thomistic cosmology can be coupled with the epigenic evolutionary unfolding of the cosmos to underpin a more realistic understanding of the universe, no one will welcome this more than the contemporary scientist and philosopher. But one thing is sure. No one today is in the market for a package deal.

The Stanford audience substantially agreed that any form of oversystematizing is suspect today, and that the fragmentary approach, especially in interdisciplinary dialogue, is the only feasible one. At this juncture, a graduate student in anthropology offered an idea which has since seemed to me of positive value. He acknowledged that since the lecture had centered attention upon Sartre and Aquinas, upon the habits of philosophers and theologians, it was inevitable that the folly of the package deal be placed upon their doorstep. But, he added, the world of science is not free from the charge of insisting upon the acceptance of systems rather than contributing viable insights. One need only turn to the later writing of Albert Einstein to see how engrossed he was with establishing the position of determinism in physical theory. Sir Julian Huxley proposes his evolutionary ethic, his religion without revelation, as a necessary consequence of scientific evolution.

So it is with many scientists today. It takes a critical thinker to disengage the scientific evolution of some men from their philosophical evolutionism which they are selling as part of an ideological system.

But even if we grant, the student added perceptively, that the second half of the twentieth century is fragmentary, that the day of the system, of the *summa,* is over, do we not have to have something to replace it? Everyone knows of the charge of overspecialization leveled against science and of the complaint that we are creating hopelessly divergent cultures within cultures. Even if it is impossible to create a worldview which will put everything together with meaning, do we not at least have to insure a living conversation, a dialogue among the disciplines?

It was at this point that a final most fruitful contribution was offered. It was the concept of professional dialogue. Built into the university idea of learning is the notion of professional criticism of research work and of inferences drawn from that research. This is mirrored by scientific journals like *Current Anthropology* which publishes research conclusions with critical evaluation by professional colleagues, and final comments by the original worker. Book reviews, symposia and conventions also play this role of intradisciplinary criticism. Is it not possible to extend this dialogue to questions which impinge upon many disciplines and thereby to increase the number and effectiveness of intellectual cross-culture discussions? Certainly, the discussion we were engaged in was such a vehicle, and out of this discussion the issues emerged clarified. The next step, perhaps, is to fashion a language which will promote communication among the intellectual cultures which, at present, are not speaking to each other.

Sartre and Aquinas are just symbols. Our intellectual and spiritual survival depends upon our avoidance of an uncritical acceptance of the extremes of the fragmentary approach of contemporary thought, on the one hand, and any form of package deal on the other. Our age is no longer in the mood for grand systems; the "picture people" have had their day and are passing. This is an age of pruning away every form of cultural baggage which can tie us to an illusion, be it in the name of science, philosophy or religion. Vatican Council II has insisted that the Church in the world today must disengage a true religious liberty, a true worship, a true realistic attitude towards the secular environment, from the world-view of an age which is no longer ours. On the other hand, the fragmentary approach, the first step of realism, is only a beginning. We must find a vehicle for spiritual solidarity and meaning to our destiny. Perhaps one of these instruments is interdisciplinary dialogue, bringing every possible insight to bear upon the urgent problems, trusting that professional competence, personal creativity and freedom will provide us with a design for the future.

V. HARVARD

Towards a Philosophy of Waste

One might truly say that today the most compelling argument for the existence of God, at least as it pertains to the amazing discoveries of scientific research, is the argument from nature's order. Never before has science so brilliantly manifested the harmonious diversities of nature, whether it be on the scale of the submicroscopic or on the grand scale of star clusters and nebulae. The more deeply research penetrates the inner recesses of matter, and the more far-reaching the discoveries of outer space, the more manifest is the lawfullness and harmonious order of the parts of the universe. Those laws and that order are unthinkable without a Designer, a Lawgiver, a providential Governor.

But evolutionary science adds another dimension to the argument from the natural order of the universe. Not only is there a magnificent order in and among things, there is an unimaginable dynamic and developmental order in their history. One can no longer be satisfied with the static order of Newton, whereby the Creator brought the universe into being, set it going, and then only tends it like a master mechanic in its status quo. *The original order, in the evolutionary picture, is no longer in existence but has been replaced by another order in process of development through space and time. Order succeeds order, and in a most orderly way. In this view of the universe, the activity of the Creator must perdure, not only to keep His creation in existence, but as Guide and Provider for the continuance of this dynamic order. If the existence of God was necessary to the old conception of the rather static order of nature, how much more is the existence of God necessary to the evolutionary order of natural development!*

LECTURE AT HARVARD UNIVERSITY, 1964
"EVOLUTION AND GOD"

67

BEFORE I left Cambridge, there was one man I desperately wanted to see: Professor George G. Simpson. In evolutionary circles, Dr. Simpson is one of a handful of scientists who have, both theoretically and in the field, established American evolutionary theory and presented it clearly to the understanding of the university mind. He is, perhaps, best known for his work on the phylogeny of the horse family, but his books and articles are, many of them, classics upon which most of the students of evolution have been introduced to the field. But more to my purposes, Dr. Simpson has played a uniquely important role in the discussions of the philosophical and theological implications of evolution. Most scientists shy away from any professional encounter with such issues, especially issues which have so controversial a history as the theory of evolution. But Dr. Simpson's writings over the last forty years of his brilliant career include some of the most candid, lucid, forceful pieces of philosophical analysis available in scientific literature, as his recent collection of essays *This View of Life* will attest. He is not a philosopher, and the rigorous methods of philosophical thought do not come easy to him, as he would be the first to admit. On occasion, he has disposed of centuries of respectable thought with a cavalier shrug. He has, on occasion, ridiculed basic Christian attitudes without the careful responsibility he so magnificently displays in his scientific work. His stubborn opposition to what appears to him uncritical ideological dogmas, his forthright style of expressing himself openly on philosophical matters, has earned him, in the eyes of some observers, the role of a villain in the evolutionary drama. But I cannot share this sentiment.

Dr. Simpson has raised some of the most perceptive philosophical problems which realistic philosophy and Christian theology must squarely face. Opposing all forms of typological thought, whether Kantian or Aristotelian, he, like his fellow biologist Sir Julian Huxley, has unflinchingly repudiated an unnecessary and invalid intrusion of the preternatural, supernatural, transcendental order of being into a self-sufficient order of nature. Vitalism, final causes, teleology, soul, hylemorphism merely sample the lexicon of concepts which he has spent his professional life trying to root out of biological thinking, simply because these terms mask the presence of an attempt to invoke a world of spirits and agents which have no place in scientific research and which are not needed for a realistic account of the workings of nature. History has shown that opposition to evolutionary thinking has arisen, in large part, from confusions of this order. Contemporary reëxamination of the Christian philosopher's "proofs" for the existence of God has suggested that the arguments are not so cogent as they once seemed to be, and that the problem of rational atheism is a very difficult one. Evolutionary humanism as a challenge to Christian belief is serious. It raises the question whether the mind can be forced with logical necessity to recognize the existence of a spiritual order of being, transcendent to but ontologically involved in the existence of the universe. Dr. Simpson has consistently replied in the negative. I had to ask him about this.

When he ushered me into his apartment, I could see the effects of his recent illness upon his face. He was hard at work editing galley proofs of an article, and I was conscious of feeling that my visit was an imposition upon his limited time and energy. Yet his kindly manner, his humility of speech, his good humor dissipated any feeling of intrusion. We were at once delightfully engaged in a discussion of the subject which he had spent his life defining: evolution. There were many points in his writings which I wanted to make sure that I grasped fully, and he patiently explained them, one by one, in his habitually lucid manner. He had read my book, and he expressed great surprise and pleasure at my extensive use of the natural-science approach in matters of philosophy and theology. He honored me with the statement that he thought my book a great step forward in theological thinking, and that if my Church took me seriously, it would effect attitudinal changes for the better. I knew that he was referring, not to dogmas of the Faith, but to the opinions of religious leaders who had so opposed evolutionary thinking these past hundred years. How painful must have been his years of teaching the convergent arguments for evolution from paleontology, genetics, ecology, physiology and biogeography, only to have students come to him and tell him that in spite of the force of the arguments they could not accept scientific evolution because it was in conflict with the teaching of the Bible, or the Catholic Church, or Christian belief. Little wonder, I thought as I heard this great scientist speak of his experiences, that he has been so critical of the "higher superstitions" of our intellectual climate!

Soon our conversation turned to the problem of order in a universe of evolving being. Discovering order in the evolutionary picture intrigued Dr. Simpson, and, although he warned about the philosophical assumptions which the concept implied, he acknowledged the orderly process of evolution. The old "static" order of the ancients is certainly a thing of the past. In its place we must be cautious not to fabricate an ideal order in nature which is illusory. The contemporary thinkers raise a valid problem when they question whether we are really discovering order in the universe or surreptitiously imposing an order upon it. "But," Dr. Simpson affirmed, "there *is* an order of organic unfolding; otherwise, we could have no scientific understanding of nature at all. Rather than speak of an orderly direction of evolution, scientists use the term 'trend' to indicate a dynamic regular process, but one which is not absolutely fixed in space and time. Dynamic order has replaced the old static order. Nature has a history, but it still obeys natural laws in unfolding that history."

Then Dr. Simpson chided me with an aside which I was to recall later as very significant. "As a matter of fact," he said, "in your book, you speak of the role of chance in evolution as being a very important one. Indeed, chance does play a role in evolution and they are mistaken who think determinism of nature rules this out." "But," he added, "I have the impression that you think this universe of ours is far more 'chancey' than it really is!" Here was an ironical switch. One hundred years ago, in the heated debates between Christian theologians and the evolutionists, the theologian accused the scientist of introducing evolutionary chance to replace the role of the Creator. Today, here was one of the foremost evolutionists of the country accusing a representative of Christian theology of thinking that the world was more filled with chance than the facts warrant! The discussion grew more serious. We were now on the threshold of one of the chief arguments of my book.

If order is such a sign and symbol of intelligent direction that it is difficult to know whether we are discovering order in nature or putting it there; and if there is an indisputable evolutionary dynamic order which prevails throughout the universe, how can a man escape the inference of the existence of an orderer, a designer, a governor responsible for the totality of this harmonious, cosmic, epigenic natural universe —whom man has ever called God? Dr. Simpson closed his eyes and remained silent. He was very tired and I regretted my taxing question, at once so difficult and so important. I had to hear him express his thought, for I admired him deeply and so thoroughly respected his thoughtfulness.

"You know," he said, smiling, and speaking very slowly now, "Father Teilhard de Chardin was a good friend of mine, and whenever he came to this country, he used to visit me. On one occasion, we went down to my ranch in the mountains near Santa Fe, and there would take long walks together. And do you know," he went on, "almost every conversation we had during those days seemed to end at this very point of our present discussion. I can only tell you what I had to tell him so many times. I find it impossible to go from this marvelous universe of ours to a transcendent order of existence. I have always venerated the order of nature as mysterious and far beyond my powers to master. But for me, my mind is enclosed in the world of nature, which I have worked with all my life. So far as I can see, the world of my existence is reason enough for its being. It is self-sufficient, independent, self-contained in its materials, agents and laws. For all we know, so the universe has always been, and so it will always be. By the only honest logical method I know, apart from cultural customs and emotional inclinations, which may at times touch us, your God who orders and governs and provides and designs is just not necessary. To me, your proof for the existence of God from the dynamic order of evolution is inconclusive. The reason: The universe is self-sufficient, infinite in time and space. Unless you can show that it is not infinite in time and space, that it hasn't always been thus and so, why should one believe that a creator and designer is necessary?"

With this straightforward statement of a great and thoughtful scientist, I had to leave Dr. Simpson. I had already tired him too much, and he had revealed to me what I had come to hear, his idea of the theological implications of his scientific work. He had no animus against theistic belief, against Christian faith, against religious hopes. My conviction, as I heard him speak of the marvels of nature, was that he is a deeply pious man, in the proper and virile sense of the word. He is profoundly respectful of the nature of which he is a part and which elicits all his veneration for its mysterious beauty. A man would be presumptuous even to hazard a guess at the deeper springs and spiritual aspirations of this scientist who has pondered so long the ways of nature. All I could think of as I returned to my quarters from my visit was how delightful an experience it was to be honored by the company and conversation of this great man, and how deep and difficult are the questions which trouble the human spirit.

A few hours later, I was still reflecting on Dr. Simpson's difficulty. The order of the universe does not demand an orderer, a designer, a transcendent being, because it has no beginning in time and space and no end. *It is self-sufficient.*

If the universe, its materials and processes, is infinite in time and space, the mind seems trapped in a self-contained, self-creative world. What does this endless process need of transcendent aid? Why invoke a designer to account for an apparently self-creative process? How does the mind break out of Dr. Simpson's evolutionary universe?

A good friend of mine, a priest doing his doctoral work in Cambridge, and who was instrumental in arranging my invitation to lecture on campus, broke in upon my reveries as I sat in my hotel room. Even before he removed his coat and made himself comfortable, I unfairly burdened him with my quandary.

"I've got a problem for you, Jim," I said.

He lit a cigarette and grew mildly attentive. I didn't bother to fill him in on my recent conversation.

"If the universe had no beginning in time and space, and no end in duration, or if you could not know whether or not the process is eternal, could you prove the existence of God?"

Jim winced at my seriousness and mustered as much concentration as could be expected on the spur of the moment.

"Why, no," he replied, hesitantly, "I don't think so. One would have to show that the universe depends on something, and if it eternally endured, had no beginning or end, it would be self-sufficient. You'd need no God, it seems to me."

"Well," I said, ignoring the fact that this kind of problem was unrelated to his present intellectual concern, "you're in trouble. There is no way of proving that the process of the unfolding of the universe is finite from anything we know in science. By the Christian faith in the revelation of Genesis, we believe that God created the universe in time, but human reason cannot demonstrate it."

He wrinkled his brow, and his whole face was a question.

"What it comes down to is this," I continued. "You are somewhat in the same rational position of agnosticism as Dr. Simpson was when I saw him an hour ago. You have your belief in God, but you are without a proof of His existence."

My friend remained silent, and glanced about the room for the refreshments. "It's too deep for me," he shrugged.

*   *   *   *   *   *

It was many weeks later that the full force of Dr. Simpson's rather incongruous remark (so it seemed to me at the time) came home to me. I was teaching a course on various philosophies of evolutionism at the Aquinas Institute of Philosophy and was in the process of comparing the thought of Henri Bergson, Sir Julian Huxley and Teilhard de Chardin. As I was rereading the essays of Sir Julian Huxley in his *Religion Without Revelation* one evening, I came across his statement: "The picture of the universe provided by modern science is of a single process of self-transformation. . . . There has been a creation of new actualities during cosmic time: it has been progressive, and it has been a self-creation." It must have been the phrases "self-transformation" and "self-creation" which recalled to mind my conversation with Dr. Simpson. Certainly, it was not the extreme evolutionary humanism of

Huxley which directly opposes Christianity and attempts to elaborate a new ethics and a new religion which reminded me of my Harvard experience. For Dr. Simpson has never presumed to be a religious leader in the name of science. It was the notion of "self-sufficiency" which called up the memory of that day in Dr. Simpson's apartment, and with that notion, his comment on my thoughts about the role of chance in the evolutionary unfolding. "I have the impression that you think this universe of ours is far more 'chancey' than it really is!" he had observed. Why had he chided me about this point? He had not rejected or criticized my religious affirmations, which he respected. He had rather singled out for comment my instinct for disorder, waste, frustration and unpredictability in this universe of ours. I was letting it play too great a role in my thought, he seemed to be saying.

Perhaps this apparent clash of instinct about disorder was important. It began to bother me, because as time went on, I was becoming worse, much worse. Whenever I lectured on the dynamic order of evolution, I was challenged. How much of that so-called dynamic order does man discover and how much does he impose? As long as science remains in the area of local cosmogonies, the laws of mass energy, gravitation, electromagnetic force and radiant energy are generally applicable. But, as R. A. Lyttleton insists, just as soon as science asks questions about the origin and development of the *cosmos as a whole,* the unity of time and space, and other cosmological questions, the resulting system is largely extrapolation far beyond accessible data. To G. J. Whitrow, W. DeSitter, R. H. Dicke, F. Kahn and many, perhaps most, modern cosmologists, the "universe" as a harmonious unity, a cosmos, is a product of the imagination and is likely to remain a pure hypothesis.

The microscopic realm of subatomic physics has been thoroughly shaken by indeterminism, and the principle of indeterminacy realistically affirms the fundamental mystery which lies at the heart of matter and energy. In the world visible to the naked eye, organic evolution is a wasteland. If successful novelty of species is the *theme* of prehistory, failure and extinction is the *counter-theme*. Individuals, species, families, whole orders and phyla of organisms have come to be, have flourished for a time, only to disappear because of limited adaptive capacity. The longer one ponders the play of orientation-opportunism of the unfolding of the biotic community, the more evolution becomes a parable of prodigality. To the Greeks, it was axiomatic that "Nature does nothing in vain." Today, the wonder is that after two billion years of such trial and error in nature's history anything but chaos could prevail.

Never before has scientific and philosophical rationalism been so severely challenged. Even the man of letters calls into question the scientist's reliance on cosmic order, for the simple reason that waste, frustration, disharmony and absurdity touch the nerve of human existence itself. The "world is crazier and more of it than we think, incorrigibly plural," proclaims Louis MacNeice. Nauseated with the contemplation, Jean-Paul Sartre laments that "from within, man keeps oozing like cheese; he is not . . ." In order to stop this "monotonous hemorrhage," man must determine himself, define himself with free, creative and personal acts. If he does not, no cosmic order, no harmony can save him, and all that remains of him is "a little bit of dirty water gurgling down the drain." These are words perhaps overcharged with drama, but as we ponder the strange unfolding of nature, and especially human history, it becomes more and more evident that there is a large element of truth in this philosophy of waste. The company of thinkers who question the illusion of order and self-sufficiency is growing daily: Heidegger, Scheler, Jaspers, Merleau-Ponty, Camus, Marcel, Brecht, Samuel Beckett. The drama of human existence, with all its crises and failures is supplanting the old world-pictures; illusory orders built upon illusions, whether scientific, philosophical or theological, are crumbling.

I finally began to see why my argument from dynamic order to an intelligent God seemed so puerile to Dr. Simpson —and why it really had no force for me either. Of course! From a picture of order alone, *there is no sense of dependence in being.* The question is not: Why this order, or why that order? The real question is: Why not nothing? It is only from the awareness of contingency, the "queasy" feeling that your existence is leaning hard on nothing, balanced upon the precipice of non-being, that calls into question your self-sufficiency. You've got to sense your creatureliness, not order, to know how dependent and insufficient you are. In fact, the very aesthetics of order may be the greatest impediment of all, obscuring this dependence of our existence by generating an illusion of self-sufficiency. No matter how infinite the time, the space, the duration of the universe, its contingency makes it so perpetually dependent, so perilously close to dropping back into nothing, that it demands the presence of the source of its being every instant to keep it in existence. That Being, upon whom all contingency rests, we call God.

As I pondered the case of evolutionary humanism, I began to wonder if I had not put my finger on the nerve of Dr. Simpson's distaste for my instinct about the role of disorder, waste and chance in the evolutionary picture. Scientific evolutionism, and humanism based upon it, prefers an orderly universe, not only to keep it in the hands of science, which is professionally understandable, but *to retain the promise of self-sufficiency*. It is precisely through its order that the universe appears self-contained; it is precisely through its orderly unfolding that it appears "self-transforming" and "self-creative." This appearance of orderly self-containment, moreover, may be so aesthetically satisfying that the deeper question "Why not nothing?" may never be asked. There is joy in the promise of perduring existence, especially if it is an orderly one; and once the mind finds self-sufficiency, it rests as with something ultimate. In the apparent self-sufficiency of the universe, a man can find more than a science of the cosmos; he can find a philosophy and a theology as well.

In all fairness to Dr. Simpson, he may have had no such thought in mind when he cautioned me about allowing to chance too dominant a role in evolution. If I were to ask him now, he no doubt would have long since forgotten the matter completely. But to me, it remains an important insight into the world of evolutionary humanism, for which I shall ever be grateful to him. For that world of scientific evolutionism is far too orderly; its expectation is overconfident. Its cosmos is too harmonious; its view is pasted together with far too many illusory extrapolations. Just pull the thread of contingency, the delicate temporal-spacial condition of the whole of it, and the imaginary cosmos will unravel into nothingness. The universe, no matter how indefinite its endurance, is constructed of stuff that is ever in need of existential support, and no amount of order and dynamism can cover for long that vulnerable spot. Creatureliness can be hopeful, expectant of promise, only so long as the Creator remains in sight.

What smashes the illusion of orderly, harmonious self-sufficiency? It is the reality of chance, unpredictability, disorder, waste, frustration and absurdity interwoven throughout the space-time unfolding of the universe and the human biography. Waste, mess, terror and frustration bring us face to face, not with self-sufficiency, but with the mystery of contingent existence. Only in the presence of this mystery does man stand solidly on the insecure ground of being a creature, sterile in meaning and impotent to last the day out on his own. Somewhere here lies the "negative theology" of a Thomas Aquinas, the mystical experience of a John of the Cross. And somewhere here lies the mystery of the Incarnation of the Son of God, of whom Paul of Tarsus says that "all things have been created through and unto Him, and He is before all creatures, and in Him all things hold together."

What becomes eminently clear to me, the more I think of it, is that the failure of evolutionary humanism, and of the atheism of men like Sir Julian Huxley, is not its impiety but its superficial rationalism. Its contemplation is not sufficiently realistic; it doesn't go deep enough. It relies too heavily upon a neat picture of the cosmos, upon a superficial, almost romantic idea of human existence. If Huxley finds his God in

80

the evolutionary cosmos, and discovers the entire meaning of human life in evolutionary nature, it is only because he has not looked at reality hard and long and squarely enough.

Atheistic humanists are picture people who are suffering a hallucination, an illusion that order prevails, and that disorder and chance are incidental. But their dream, their vision of a self-sufficient cosmos, is threatened by the stark realism of the drama people, who suck the bitter ashes of frustration and daily breathe the stench of death. The atheist has appropriated the old theistic argument from order and demonstrates that God is irrelevant. Paradoxically, the theist has appropriated the old atheistic argument from chance and disorder, and demonstrates that it is unthinkable that creatures could hang long on the thread of contingency, on the threshold of nothing, without being sustained by the hand of Him who placed them there. Our crying need today is not for a more refined cosmology of order; we desperately need a more realistic philosophy of waste.

VI. NEW ORLEANS

The Terror of History

I sensed this most acutely one day in San Francisco on my way to a trial run for a television program. A very kind gentleman, whom I had never met before, picked me up at my hotel to drive me to the studio. After the usual amenities, we were about to drive off when suddenly he stopped. "Something wrong?" I asked. "Yes," he replied, smiling apologetically, "your seat-belt is not fastened." There was nothing about the day, the lovely Bay area, the occasion, and certainly nothing about this generous gentleman's manner that accounts for the sudden interior rebellion that overtook my spirit. It was as though I had been struck with a lightning bolt, and I felt the shock of almost divine illumination which was both blinding and crystal clear. It was the realization of the oppression which is generated by a kind of seat-belt spirituality, the compulsion to be tucked in securely so that the fears of the future cannot touch you.

It seemed to me, with the lucidity of prophecy, that this was the blight of the age, the neurotic panic to take the terror out of history. I had no reason to gainsay the reliability of the Yale studies; it was just that I refuse to suborn my freedom, my creativity and my personality to a statistic. I demand my right to jump into a car to take a ride with no thought of whether my nose will be smashed on the windshield. To live dangerously and be free to converse with someone in the back seat. To take a curve without the strong, scientific, impersonal arm holding me about the midriff. I know that it is unscientific, irrational, subjective and uncircumspect, and I do not for a moment wish to advise another to follow in the footsteps of my folly, but I then, at that very moment, vowed never to fasten my seat-belt again. And if it were not for those severe commands, sanctioned by charming smiles, which I have had from irresistible airline hostesses, my vow would be intact today.

LECTURE AT XAVIER UNIVERSITY, NEW ORLEANS, 1965
"EVOLUTION AND THE FUTURE OF MAN"

ANY doubt that my lecture on evolution and the future of man had a unique significance for the Xavier University audience was dissipated by the first question from one of the 1,200 Negro students on campus. In the face of the integration attempts at "Ol' Miss" a year ago, the marches on Atlanta a few weeks ago, and the then-current strife of Bogalusa, merely symptomatic of the social upheaval of integration throughout the nation, my lecture had a detached, theoretical quality. Certainly, the lexicon I was using was devoid of the ring of rhetoric: the fossil record, natural selection, genetics, taxonomy, physical anthropology, cosmic order, epigenesis, biopoesis, polygenism, biogeography, Australopithecines. Nothing reminiscent of sit-ins, marches, violence, Ku Klux Klan, death, injustice, hatred about these abstractions. That the evolutionary theme in biology and anthropology does not severely challenge either realistic philosophy or the Christian revelation may have surprised some but the key interest of this alert and intelligent student body was triggered from another, unexpected quarter.

I had said, in passing, that the world into which Darwin and evolutionary science had led us was a new one, one in which history, space-time contingency, was an essential, not an incidental, factor. Henceforth, no philosophy, no theology of man could claim to be authentic and realistic which disregarded or minimized the meaning of history, of evolutionary development. Moreover, cultural anthropology today recognizes that *Homo sapiens* is unique in the animal kingdom. Man is the only animal that designs and fashions its own niche, its own future. He has evolved a principle of freedom, creativity and personality by which he, like no other animal, must not only adapt to but also refashion his surroundings in order to survive. Man is essentially a history-making animal, and failure freely and personally to create his tomorrow will expose him to extinction.

The student who rose to speak, like all the others present, had watched me place human existence solidly within the context of contingent history. If there is meaning to human existence, it must be found here. As he slowly and quietly set forth his question, earnestly but without the slightest indication of impatience or anxiety, I marvelled. "If space-time history is of the essence of man, and the making of history his free, creative and personal prerogative and obligation, how is it possible to tolerate and to justify the suffering and annihilation of so many peoples who suffer and are annihilated for the simple reason that their geography sets them in the pathway of history, that they are, for example, neighbors of empires in the state of permanent expansion?"

He had not asked about the justice and charity which is owed to a race and not given. He asked for no prognosis about the Negro-white cultural differences which are being reported daily in the papers. He was not asking for an explanation of evil in the world, for I am sure that he, like most of the student body, accepted the Judaeo-Christian revelation concerning the presence of evil in the world. Suffering which

comes from personal irresponsibility is unfortunate but understandable, and can be corrected. His question was far
deeper and touched the heart of my presentation. How do
you find meaning in the mystery of human history which
seems to unfold with inescapable inevitability against the very
creative, personal freedom which inspires man to plan his
future? Is man's history determined with necessity? Is his
history-making role only an illusion? If man is necessarily an
historical animal and if the greater picture of his unfolding is
inevitable, how can he find enough meaning to understand,
or at least to tolerate, his future? How can he learn to live
with the tomorrow over which he has no control, from which
he has no appeal? In a word, how can man take the terror
out of history? The question was as perceptive as it was fair.

It is a fact of greatest moment that man, almost from the
first discovery that he exercises a measure of freedom and
creativity, has ever attempted to protect this prerogative by
throwing up limits to the exercise of that freedom. Moral and
religious traditions, customs and habits, at once stabilize and
fix the patterns of human activity for the future. It is as
though primitive man did not trust his freedom and creativity, lest the good gained by the last creative breakthrough
would be lost by irresponsible neglect or forgetfulness. As a
consequence, early men, almost without exception, fixed their
existence firmly in the immutability and sanction of the
divine.

Mircea Eliade shows, in his remarkable analysis *The Myth
of the Eternal Return,* how the language and literature of the
oldest civilizations and most primitive tribes display this
spiritual attitude towards reality. For primitive man, reality

is a function of the imitation of a celestial archetype. This reality is conferred through participation in the symbolism of the "center," whereby important cities, men, history of the tribe or civilization are associated with the "center of the world." And finally, rituals and significant profane gestures acquire meaning attributed to them, and materialize that meaning only because they deliberately repeat such acts in imitation of the gods, heroes or ancestors. In short, every tribe, every civilization, has its most important patterns of meaningful human activity, not from human freedom and creativity, but from the gods. Immutable (and thus not free) canons of behavior are thus formulated within which all the contingencies of history, and all the vicissitudes of daily life must be interpreted. With the same energy that man discovers means of designing and improving his tomorrow, he attempts to guarantee this improvement against the ravages of history by securing it in the celestial plan.

The innovator, especially in moral and religious matters (and every question of meaning is ultimately moral and religious), is always looked upon with suspicion. A prophet is not without honor save in his own country. But if this innovation proves salutary and a fountain of blessings for posterity, the man once held in derision and reproach may become a hero, a founder and a father of a new race. Ultimately, he will take his place among the gods, and his freedom and creativity will be canonized into immutable, divinely sanctioned rules. And so the process goes, all in an effort to take the terror out of history. It was a mere step from this deliberate association of important human activity with the celestial archetype to the annulment of time itself. For ancient traditions, without exception, defended themselves to the utmost of their powers against the novelty and irreversibility which history entails.

Thus for the Babylonians, Egyptians, Hebrews, Iranians, for almost every primitive people, the existence of man in the profane cosmos is regarded as a "fall." The reason is that the historical memory, the recalling of events that fall short of the celestial archetype (and all historical existence does), and the recollection of personal failure and frustration, is intolerable. They have to be wiped out, annihilated. This is done by some form of renewal or regeneration of time. Almost every people has its form of New Year, its religious ritualistic celebration of a return to the celestial center, the transcendent existence of the world beyond the ravages of profane time and place.

Thus the terror of history, the explanation of disorder, waste, frustration, misfortune and calamity, finds its key in the "eternal return."

It is easy to see this theme taken up and rationalized in the Greek and Roman philosophies. It is notable that Aristotle's philosophy of nature, in which he so thoroughly repudiates the "other-worldiness" of Platonic forms, treats the cosmos ultimately in an untimely, unhistorical fashion. All temporal-spacial nature is governed by the celestial spheres, and individual history is swallowed up by the eternal essences. For him, as for all the Greek philosophers, and all the medieval systems which were based upon the Greek insight, time remained incidental to the ultimate explanation of existence. For the ancients, whether ordinary or sophisticated, and for traditional cosmic views up to recent times, the terror of history was absorbed by this celestial economy. As long as the myth of the eternal return prevailed, history had no intrinsic value, no inherent meaning, no imminent intelligibility. History was, in fact, non-existent.

But the contemporary mind has repudiated this myth, and has replaced it with another: the myth of the shifting sands. For early man, human history had no real value, no real existence, but for contemporary man, human history is the only thing of value. To the latter, man *is* his historical unfolding, and if there is any meaning to human existence, it has to be found within history itself. The celestial archetypes, the regeneration of time, the aspiration of man to take the terror out of history by dissolving it into a world of transcendent place and mythical time, are scorned by twentieth-century man as totally illusory.

What, then, of the reality of history's misfortunes, of all the waste, the frustrations, the failure, the disorder, the contradictions of profane history? How can man explain to himself the meaning of tomorrow's threat to his well-being? Without the celestial archetypes, without the transcendent "other-world," in which he once hoped to participate, what can he say in the face of temporal contingency and disaster? Contemporary man's answer is simple. Man can make his own history, his own tomorrow. He can find meaning for history, just as he can find meaning for triangles and circles: he fashions history freely, creatively, personally, to his own tastes. He needs no archetypes, no figment of eternal return, no symbolism of regeneration of time. These are but ideas, rationalizations which man, in the midst of panic, thought he needed. Crush these illusions by the simple phenomenology of cosmic and human unfolding. Take hold of the future by making your tomorrow what you wish. Cut away the cultural baggage of the myth of the eternal return, and face up to the reality of the shifting sands of time. Take your instruction from the past, rectify the failures of the present, and build a new and better future. This is the answer of many historicists today.

The traditional reply is well known. The "realism" of historicism is also a myth, and its freedom and creativity is equally illusory for nearly the whole of the human race. For the attempts of man to organize the future in terms of freedom and creativity have shown that such organization has fallen to the lot of a few, who, having the power to control creativeness, have restricted and subjugated the powerless, thus increasing the terror of *their* history. The only chance for effective freedom and personal creativity, argues the traditionalist, is to work from within the bounds of some form of celestial archetype, some form of eternal return. Within this orientation, there is more freedom, more personal creativity, less terror in history than in the contemporary solution. Contemporary man, says the traditionalist, shows himself to be neither a free being, nor a personal creator of history. The myth of the shifting sands is more illusory than the myth it strenuously opposes.

What might easily be lost in our contemporary dilemma is the fact that man does not have to choose between these two myths. He does not have to choose between saying that history has no intrinsic value and saying that history has no transcendent value and meaning. There is a third option which has been given to man through the Judaeo-Christian revelation; it is that of *salvation history*. For the Hebrews, and for the Christian tradition, history is regarded as theophany. Yet history retains an intrinsic value. God is accomplishing His plan in man's time and in man's space. This is a one-way process, and the persons, places and events have intrinsic value because they are, themselves, the very working out of the divine plan. Historical events can be tolerated, even enthusiastically embraced, because they contribute essentially to final happiness. Directly ordered by God, history becomes a series of theophanies. Time is essential. Yet it is irreversible, not eternally repeated. History has value in and of itself, but its ultimate significance is revealed by God. Terror is alleviated, not by nullifying time, but by interpreting temporal unfolding by the eschatology of divine fulfillment.

Christ, the God-incarnate, the redeemer of all creation, is the end of time. One day, time will cease. Indeed, with the Incarnation, the end of time has already been accomplished. History is the unique occasion, the stage, as it were, on which each individual enters fully into the drama of salvation history, and works out his role in the divine plan. In this view, a transcendent orientation safeguards freedom and personal creativity against the tyranny of the few. Yet each man must freely, creatively and personally work out his salvation through the contingent circumstances of his own daily existence. The infinite difference which separates this view from both the myth of the eternal return and the myth of the shifting sands is that whereas they attempt to remove the terror of history by an act of rationalization, Judaeo-Christian theology of history arises from, and ever depends upon, an act of supernatural faith.

Paradoxically, however, salvation history as the Judaeo-Christian answer to the terror of tomorrow is a thread of hope which is ever being lost by each age. Personal faith tends to become identified with the age; revealed theophanies tend to become identified with local cultures. The grand, sublime sweep of salvation history is entrapped by a people, a place or a time, and some form of the myth of the eternal return is revived. Christianity ever tends to become identified with Christendom. To the contemporary mind, so sensitive to the realism of evolutionary anthropology and the accent on historicity, the Christian tradition is essentially an anti-historical attitude. The great scandal to modern times is that the Christian revelation has become so identified with antiquated times and places and cultures that it appears totally irrelevant to our age.

The reason is not far to see. Christianity has not yet responded with vigor to an essentially historical view of salvation. It is still very much in bondage to some form of eternal return. For a great majority of Christians, even in this day of evolutionism, historicism and existentialism, history is not a theophany. History, for most Christians, is not something to be embraced; it is something to be feared and repudiated. It is something which is "secular" and "profane" and therefore something which should be "risen above." Evidence for this is found both in traditional teachings on the spiritual life and in pastoral practice.

In the Roman Catholic Church, for example, both seminary and secular education is largely based upon the theological synthesis of the Scholastics and the Fathers, which, in turn, is essentially Greek in philosophical orientation. Platonic archetypes, Aristotelian "essences" and a cyclical view of temporal regeneration still govern the blueprint of Christian life. The revelation of Christ is structured into a grand system which transforms the timely into the timeless, and threatens to identify salvation history with a single cultural ideal corresponding to Christendom during the Middle Ages. Thus Catholic education, until very recently, has passed along a tradition of "other-worldliness," a view of the universe and the meaning of human existence in which space and time play no essential roles. Its thought has been fundamentally a-historical (perhaps anti-historical), witnessed by the fact that in all its theological and philosophical research, the philosophy and theology of history are still in an embryonic and exploratory stage.

Of recent date, however, Christianity has been warned about its vulnerability to lapse into some idyllic form of eternal return, its temptation to remove the terror of history by listening to the deceptive lyrics of "celestial harmonies." New religious phenomenologies have emerged to deliver the kernel of Christ's Gospel from the husklike accretions of former cultures. Well known is the effort of Max Scheler, for example, to free the revelation of salvation history from the theories of Aquinas or Kant or Schleiermacher. A convert to the Catholic Church, he finally abandoned the Church because he did not think that the essential experience of Divinity and the authentic experience of Christ could be conveyed through the concepts and language of Thomism. This theological tradition, so authoritatively encouraged by the Church throughout the first half of this century as a blueprint for seminary and secular Catholic education, was embraced because of the realism of its insights. But Thomism, as a system, has one very basic shortcoming: it is a view of the universe and of man in which history is incidental. Now if there is one question which the twentieth century has clearly and squarely put to Christianity it is this: What is the meaning of history, of the existential, personal unfolding of human life? Is history incidental? Or, rather, is the drama of Christ's life among us *essentially* historical? It is the test of authentic Christianity in our times. If Christianity belongs to the "other-world," then it is irrelevant. But if history has an intrinsic value, as evolutionism, and historicism and existentialism insist, then Christianity must abandon the myth of the eternal return and take its stand in salvation history.

Vatican Council II is the beginning of the answer of the Catholic Church to this question of the century. When it had finished its work, it had produced sixteen documents on a broad spectrum of important subjects. It is yet too early to assess the effect of these declarations, and to foresee all the attitudinal changes, inside and outside the Church, which have been initiated by this council. But every decree and declaration attests to the fact that the Church defines herself and her role in terms of human history. The single, unmistakable inference which must be drawn from the Catholic Church's self-study is that human history is a theophany.

The redemptive action of Christ is found only in man's history; it is man's time which has been redeemed. The whole thrust of Vatican Council II is so to place the Church of Christ in the world as to consecrate the secular world by the theophany of history. Profane history is intrinsically valuable because it is at one and the same time salvation history. Contemporary evolutionists, historicists and existentialists have underscored an important reality for Christianity. History belongs essentially to the very definition of man, and no philosophy or theology of man is authentic which devaluates this developmental unfolding. The salutary effect of contemporary realism has been to destroy the myth of eternal return, and to force Christians to rediscover, to purify and to elaborate their precious heritage of the only theology of history which can remove the terror without removing time—salvation history.

* * * * * *

"Nothing under the sun is new . . . for it hath already happened in the ages which have gone before us." Solomon was not in a very festive mood when he recorded these words in *Ecclesiastes*. Why do we spend so much time trying to take the fear out of tomorrow? The wise men of old have ever thought to ground their assurances, their generalizations, upon a timelessness which appears to neutralize the unexpected event. Camels are camels are camels . . . So speaks tradition.

Yet there is illusion in this attempt to tuck all of our day into such categories of "that's the way things are." Nothing in physical creation escapes the imprint of space and time. To be so immersed is the very mark of creatureliness. Space and time are not incidental; they are of the stuff of things.

You cannot say what a camel is, what a salamander is, what a man is—even what the wisdom and providence of God might be—unless you can interpret the intrinsic value of space and time.

How the human spirit can be drawn forth by a slight encounter with the timely of which it is so deeply a part! Such tiny, momentary intrusions of the circumstances of my day, which could not possibly cause the slightest ripple in the calm, lucid waters of the sophisticated science and wisdom of the ages, *are* the newness of things. They belong uniquely to me as a person and they condition my tomorrows with both fear and expectation. My thoughts and my love, without which I would simply drop back into nothing, draw fresh exhilaration and swift movement from this momentary newness of things.

Yet I could not get the quiet, detached voice of the Xavier University student out of my mind. We are willing to leave the terror in history, to admit that our tomorrows have intrinsic value, to expend free, personal and creative effort with courage. But what of Selma and Birmingham and Bogalusa? The marches of Saul and David had meaning from an act of faith in Yahweh's plan; whence comes the meaning of our marches? We are anxious to avoid the illusions of the tradition of our times, the myth of eternal return, and the myth of the shifting sands. But from which direction will come our prophet of salvation history? We hear from one camp that time is nothing, and that we shall have our "pie in the sky." From another camp, we hear that time is everything, and that there is no expectation but what we, ourselves, create in our tomorrows. What you tell us is new and strange: that our time is at the heart of things, yet Christ has redeemed that very time, and awaits our entry into the drama of His life. How is this to be accomplished?

This is deep mystery. I must think on it.

VII. ANN ARBOR

A Piece of Pumpernickel

I am a Roman Catholic and I believe in the community of saints, both in heaven and on earth. I believe that the happy spirits in heaven can and sometimes do assist by their intercessory power, the spirits in this vale of tears. I have heard that St. Christopher is good on the highways, that St. Jude is terrific with impossible cases, and that St. Anthony is the one you turn to when lost articles fail to show up. But I will tell you something. I do not think that St. Anthony finds things for you, like lost golf balls, for instance. You know who finds lost golf balls? Impoverished golfers who haven't the cash to buy new ones every day, and caddies on their days off, so that they can wash them up and sell them. Why do they find them, when others don't? I'll tell you why. Because they look and look and look until they look in the right place where the ball was all the time. Well, then, where does St. Anthony come in? All I can see is that somehow through an appeal of the spirit, like the encouragement of a gesture from a lover, there is motive generated, motive which urges a man to look and look and look until he looks in the right place, where the ball was all the time. Now to say that the saints are thereby unnecessary, that St. Anthony is just superstitious baggage in the business of human affairs, is to make the claim that the gesture of the lover is irrelevant.

LECTURE AT THE UNIVERSITY OF MICHIGAN, 1965
"EVOLUTION AND COSMIC ORDER"

ONCE you have made your way in the world and have strenuously spent years carving your niche, hesitate prayerfully before you return home. You will not only find that everything has shrunken to Tom Thumb size—the streets shorter, your back yard too small to play in, the business section just a handful of storefronts—you will find that this tiny place will swallow you up. You may have conquered giants in other lands, but the mysterious fears of this land of your youth remain unconquered. You may have banqueted with kings and princes in other places, but around your family supper table they nod to you, just as gently unimpressed as they ever were. So you have found yourself, and know who you are? Here is the test. Walk along the street on which you were born.

Accepting a lecture at the University of Michigan was like going home after an odyssey of thirty years. Ann Arbor was not my birthplace, but the University was my intellectual home. It all really started here. Here I studied for the first time. Here I tasted college life and friendships; here I learned to revere the life of the professor, the scientist, the writer. Here I first listened to music, watched plays, studied wildlife in the field, followed college athletics, became enamored of biological evolution and human ecology, discussed ideas until the early hours, learned a profession. But more than that, it was here at the University of Michigan that an idea was generated which was to set the guidelines for my entire life to this very moment. It was here, in my senior year back in 1939, that I freely and personally chose to face a mysterious, unknown future with an act of belief. Here, I became a Catholic. Nothing was to be the same again, for destiny is shaped by one or two decisions in our life; to this day, all that I am is somehow but the projection of those days in Ann Arbor. Yet, like every return home, the new sun reveals old illusions. This visit was no exception.

During the almost thirty years that have passed, through my years as a Dominican religious, a student of philosophy and theology, a professor of philosophy, a lecturer in the United States and in Europe, I have tried to put the fragments of that story together. And every time I tell it to myself, it unfolds in a different fashion. At times, one event, one person, seems central; at other times, new faces and new factors are integral to the drama.

It all began with a piece of pumpernickel bread at Metzger's German-American inn. It was feverish-study time in my senior year; and an occasional trip downtown to a restaurant for dinner was a treat. On this particular late afternoon, I had dinner with a zoologist friend of mine, Bill Bujak, an energetic doctoral candidate who was then finishing his work on a project in animal ecology. We sat in silence there at Metzger's, listening to Strauss waltzes amidst the subdued conversations of the early dinner-hour patrons. Our waitress's name was "Gigi," as we were to learn from the decorous card neatly folded on our table. The couple at the next table were excited about an art show they had just attended. The one doing all the talking couldn't get over "how philosophical Edward spoke" and "how well Georgie played the guitar." Suddenly, Gigi appeared, and with impeccable structuring on her little pad, she had taken our orders. As she finished writing, she turned to me and asked: "What kind of bread would you like?"

"White bread, please," I replied.

"And you, sir?" she asked my friend.

"I'll have pumpernickel bread," Bill said.

The music played on. Suddenly, Bill spoke. I could tell that he was in a serious mood, for he wore an intense, somewhat embarrassed look as he launched his question.

"Do you mind if I become a bit personal?" he began.

"Not at all," I answered. "Fire away."

"Why did you order white bread?" Bill was smiling now.

"Because," I replied, somewhat surprised at the trivial turn the conversation seemed to take, "I *like* white bread; just as in your choice, you ordered pumpernickel because you *like* pumpernickel."

"Not quite," he replied firmly. "I ordered pumpernickel bread because it's *good* bread. There's a difference."

Scores of trivial incidents like this one occur in our lives every day. Yet at just the right time, a passing remark by the right person can be indelibly inscribed upon our hearts like a parable. I was not so sure about the litany of "good" things you could say about pumpernickel bread in contrast to white bread. The point which bore its way into my consciousness more and more as the days wore on was that there can be an infinite distance between the world of what is objectively good, and right and true, and the world of what we like. The former is an order which is largely given and has to be discovered; the latter is often the imposition of the self upon all that we know and see and think and do. How could you disengage yourself from that which was merely "what you like" and attach yourself to "what was good?" It was an issue which I met in every discussion, every class, every cultural experience. Whether it was law, sociology, poetry, biology, movies, friendships, religion, the question was there. To my mind, a man must above all discover the objective order of things. In each major moment of decision, one has to dissociate personal taste and convention from the truth of the way things stand. Subjective preference may coincide with objective excellence at times; then again, it may not. In all things, however, the objective order was to take first place. So it seemed to me then, and it was by no means a simple matter to discover this order, especially in matters close to the heart. In the main, my studies in science, literature, education and social studies compounded the complexity of the question because of the plethora of factual analyses we were required to master.

Yet in my reading, a unique blueprint was beginning to emerge. I began to take notice of a handful of writers who seemed to be wrestling with this same issue of systematic objectivity: Mortimer Adler in the philosophy of law; Hilaire Belloc and G. K. Chesterton in literature; Christopher Dawson in sociology; Robert Hutchins in education; Henri Fabre in natural history. Quite by accident, it seemed, these men— and others were to be slowly added to the list—were convergent experiences in my senior days of soul-searching for a philosophy of life which would pull things together for me. Before I graduated, I was then convinced, I had to find a philosophy of order which would do this for me. That systematic view of a cosmic harmony which intellectually embraced the totality of my university experience was the realism of two philosophers who became the lights of my life in those days: Etienne Gilson and Jacques Maritain. To them, there was a cosmic order, a human order, an artistic and moral order, an orientation in which personal taste has free, but not tyrannical, play. Here was the synthesis I was searching for.

Strange as it may sound, I did not, for quite some time, associate this synthesis with the Roman Catholic Church. After all, though Maritain was a Catholic, Hutchins was a Protestant and Adler was a Jew. I was looking for binding ideas, not a faith to believe in. The fact that the ideas I found most attractive belonged to scientists, artists and philosophers who were also members of the Catholic Church did not strike me as odd. I did not, at first, know how to respond to a religious instinct; my only concern was intellectual. I belonged to no church, and that dimension of my personality had not awakened during those days of intense study and reading. I read, and pondered, and read some more—until life began to swim and I lost my spiritual bearings. How, in such a quandary, does a man find himself, his own personal commitment, his own niche? I had no idea even how to go about answering such a question.

This new dimension of my spirit opened up a very blue Monday. I was living on Hill Street at the time, and I was returning from campus after an examination in one of my English-language courses. My effort had been miserable, and I was in a deep funk. Suddenly, as I walked, a shiny object on the sidewalk, something like a dime, caught my eye. I stooped to pick it up. It was a Catholic medal. Long ago, one of the kids on my block wore a chain with several of these medals dangling around his neck. They jingled as he ran, I remembered, and from those early days, I had learned to regard such practices as superstitious folly. As I drew my arm back to sail the medal into the grove of aspen trees across the street, a thought struck me. Why are you doing this? Is this another precipitous reaction to a culture which does not fit the aesthetics of your personal taste? I pocketed the medal and took it home with me.

In my room on Hill Street, I had a powerful pair of binoculars which I often used on bird hikes. If the binoculars are reversed, they become an effective magnifying glass. I cleaned off the medal and studied it through the binoculars. I saw, for the first time, the unforgettable image of Mère de la Croix. About this figure of the Mother of God I could make out the words, "O Mary, conceived without sin, pray for us who have recourse to thee." This medal, I was to learn, was the highly revered Catholic "Miraculous Medal." Who can describe the deepest movements of the human spirit? One cannot talk about these matters even to one's closest friends. Only this can I say. With that discovery of the medal, the image of Mary, the suggestion of her divine role, the thought of intercessory prayer took root in my soul.

The deepest need for recourse to spiritual enlightenment struck me with such force during the following days that I became engulfed by a strange silence. I ate little, and missed several classes; I was not ill, but I was intensely quiet and very alone. Not a little consolation was the fact that my newly found intellectual guides were also profoundly reverent towards the religious dimension represented by the Lady on this medal. I think I began to pray. Then, slowly, a new kind of awareness, deep strength and joy came to me. I had come out of the forest, where only the sound of the phoebe was heard, into the warm light of a new day. Since those mysterious moments of awakening, there has been no night.

*   *   *   *   *   *

My lecture on evolution and cosmic order was well received, and the questions and discussion were very stimulating. But the general impression which the event had upon a great number of people was one of bewilderment, I think. It was not that they were disappointed with what they heard. It was rather that they had not fully expected my approach to reality. I had seen that expression on the faces of the members of the Catholic Philosophical Association at the convention held in Denver a few months before. One philosopher had left shaking his head, saying, "He is no longer a Thomist!" As if that had anything to do with the issue. The question is simply whether the universe and all its parts are unfolding in an evolutionary fashion, man and his spirit included, and what are the consequences of this. If being a Thomist had anything to do with it, the least he could have done would have been to remember what St. Thomas said in a similar situation: "The philosopher is not concerned with the opinions of other philosophers, he is only concerned with how the truth of things stands."

So too, here at Michigan, I had an image which did not prepare the listener for what he heard. I was a convert Catholic priest, a Dominican raised in one of the most professional, thoroughgoing Thomistic traditions. I was a former professor of philosophy in the Angelicum University in Rome, and presently professor of the philosophy of nature in the Aquinas Institute of Philosophy in River Forest, Illinois, an image of the most traditional approach to reality which a man's past could reflect. I must, therefore, view the universe of nature and the world of man in the traditional cosmic setting where harmonious order of all things, cosmic, human and divine, prevailed. For one of this tradition, science, philosophy and theology must reflect the symphonic harmonies of the celestial spheres. This, I am sure, many fully expected to hear. But they did not.

Instead, they heard that the microcosm is fundamentally indetermined, that the world of life and of man is evolving in large part by chance, that a cosmic harmony or a universe as a whole is largely a product of the imagination. They heard that cosmic design is hopelessly lost to contemporary science, that there are no intrinsic, unalterable, absolute laws of nature. They heard that space-time contingency and evolutionary unfolding are essential, not incidental, conditions of cosmic prehistory, human history and personal biography; that natural law is developmental and cannot sustain a personal ethic except in the most general sense of orientation; and that, finally, religious belief cannot be tied unalterably to any one view of nature, any one metaphysic, any one psychology or any particular school of theology. In short, they heard that the world-picture of centuries past has been shattered, that no new twentieth-century world synthesis has emerged to replace it, and that world pictures are giving way to interpersonal

105

drama. Upon the latter, human belief and the new theologies are being constructed, and this perforce by reason of the evolutionary, space-time, epigenetic dimension of all reality.

Of course, put in capsule form, this summation of twentieth-century thinking on the evolutionary question sounds far more revolutionary and catastrophic than it really is. There is a great deal of dynamic order in the universe; it is just far more indetermined and unpredictable than we imagined. There is a natural, lawful, orderly unfolding in the organic realm; there is just a much larger play of chance than we once thought. There is a natural orientation in the inclinations of man which provide norms of situation adjustment, but man cannot elaborate rules of conduct exclusively from these changing points of orientation. What is most revolutionary about it all is that past cultures had placed undue value upon these illusory orders. Now we are discovering that we must carefully distinguish the Christian revelation from the cosmologies, the ontologies and the psychologies which once underpinned it.

I finally managed to disengage myself from the last remnants of the discussion group and left the auditorium. The night Ann Arbor air was soft, and I walked alone in the direction of my old rooming house on Hill Street. As I reflected upon the evening, I suddenly regretted having made a statement which came back to me very clearly now. I regretted it because I had not fully known what I was trying to express. I had not thought the matter through myself, and taken on face value, my statement could have grossly misrepresented the truth. I had said that it had taken me but two years to find the Catholic Church, but it had taken me another twenty-five years to find Christ. That was certainly a startling statement for a Dominican priest to make, for it sounds as though a life calculated to be the quickest, surest and most thorough vocation in the following of Christ was, in fact, a serious impediment. Nothing could be further from the truth.

But we are, all of us, in each of our personal vocations, attempting to discover Christ in our life. This search never ends; it is the heart of the mystical life. If the Incarnation of God in my history, the redemption and ascension of Jesus Christ is the one event which is decisive in all my life work —indeed the meaning of all existence—then the decision to enter into that event must be mine and mine alone. It cannot be confused with the aesthetic harmony of a system; the genial companionship of an organization; the nobility of a work; the assent of our peers—or even the cosmic harmony of the spheres. Christ attaches himself to no language, to no system, to no world-picture, to no culture. But it took me many years to separate a beautiful, but partly illusory, system of thinking about Christ and His revelation, which has variously been called Christian philosophy and Christian theology, from the simple drama of Christ's life to which we must personally respond.

Even as I walked the streets of the University, where my first sincere step of belief had been taken, I knew that the way a man finds Christ has to be his very own. The way I found Him was not the only way. It was not necessarily the best way (after all, what could *that* mean?), nor would it be my way today. For the very order which so enthralled me during my student days, I repudiated as largely illusory in

107

my lecture tonight. Now, as I returned to the place of my conversion to Christianity, I came full circle in my view of reality. Adler, the philosopher of law, who once captivated me with his love for St. Thomas's insights, now seemed to me but a brilliant dialectician. Now Hutchins' educational views seemed quaintly medieval and ineffectual. To me now, Dawson's social thought seemed dated, laborious and unnecessarily pedantic. Chesterton's witty, journalistic apologetic is quickly tiresome, and Belloc's lucid prose is noisy and, at times, bigoted. Maritain, the theologically orientated philosopher, came too late upon the relevance of historicity. And so it has gone with nearly all of my heroes of the 1930's. They were heroes of cosmic order and the grand synthesis in which man could find himself and feel at home. My world, the world of the latter half of the twentieth century, had become fragmented and disjointed.

As I walked, I found myself approaching the spot where I had found the Miraculous Medal. It was equally clear to me, as I retraced my steps, that the revelation of Christ cannot be attached to the finding of medals any more than to the finding of champions of cosmic order. The world-view of Belloc, Chesterton, Dawson, Adler, Hutchins and Maritain, so harmonious and orderly, had passed. Nor is there anything in the order of things which demands Miraculous Medals. Just as I could no longer place much stock in my old intellectual guides, so I no longer could muster much patience with medal carrying. But to leave the matter here, to speak as though the past had betrayed me, would be grossly unfair.

It is not the events which happen in time and space which

make all the difference, as though the cosmos were providentially unfolding like a giant machine, grinding out human destiny in accordance with unalterable laws. It is the value which you, as a free and creative person, assign to the things that happen. It is not that pumpernickel bread, or Belloc, or the Miraculous Medal, wrought the turn of my destiny. You can dispense medals by the thousands and nothing will happen. It is the value, the meaning of the role which I freely, creatively and personally gave to the medal at the time, that afternoon, in this place here on Hill Street. Divine providence concerns less a change of place and time, and more a change of heart. This is important. Too many look for the intentions of the Holy Spirit with cosmic inevitability in the way a raindrop falls down a window pane. This is superstition, like Russian roulette, and can lead to catastrophe. Divine provision is the guarantee of the courageous choice of a great heart.

It was this lesson which took me so long to learn, even in a vocation best suited to find Christ the redeemer. You can acknowledge what harmony and order that you find in the cosmos, but you cannot believe in it. By the same token, there cannot be a supreme ontology or psychology or theology which is sufficiently necessary and finished to bind a man to a belief in the incarnate God. The cosmic view of St. Thomas and the Middle Ages, one in which Maritain and Gilson and Chesterton and Adler and Hutchins found so many impressive insights, attached them to a belief only so long as the culture gave that value to the view. I am not saying that a world-view is not an important instrument of a man's belief.

109

I am saying that the world-picture is important only so long as we give it that value. We believe in Christ, not in a world-view. Christ attaches Himself, not to a system, nor to a picture of reality, nor to a culture, but to a piece of bread.

But even here, it need not be pumpernickel. For to this day, I still order white bread—because I like white bread.

VIII. MIAMI

The Strange World of Father Teilhard

In the middle of the twentieth-century space age, we no longer gaze out upon the heavens, the celestial spheres, as though we were contemplating a divine cosmos. We are no longer completely at home in a world which is ours, one which we can take in with a sweeping glance. Today, man peers, with squinted eyes, into the darkness with only pin-points of light to illumine his way. His existence is not unlike that of the oceanographer in a submarine, exploring uncharted waters by throwing out a beam of light and recording what comes into view. With creative genius, man can discover new techniques, like radar and sonar, to broaden his range of experience. He can infer, quite legitimately, that there is much more beyond his range of vision which is similar to what he sees. He is aware also that new varieties of fish, coral and seaweed are coming into being and, after a fleeting existence, passing away; the panorama of aquatic flora and fauna is constantly changing. He is confident that he will ever expand his range of vision. But he is also aware, more and more, that what he sees is only a tiny fragment of the vast unexplored sea—and so it will probably remain.

Thus the problem is posed: in the mystery of cosmic epigenesis, the gradual fragment of unfolding being within our intellectual grasp, can we discover any meaning, any significant direction of this evolution in time and space? If space-time contingency is the very condition of the reality we know, if finalities are themselves slowly opening up with novelty and surprise, how are we to find a key with which to unlock the mystery? Can we look out upon the universe and find a "mirror of divinity"? Or must we say that what we see is so basically immersed in contingency that being is leaning hard on nothing—and nothing is just what God

111

is not? *Is nature so unfinished that it is no more than a remote intrinsic orientation, a direction which is only a hint? Must the wayfarer be content to make his way with impromptu notes and great courage amidst the thicket of contingent history?*

LECTURE AT THE UNIVERSITY OF MIAMI, 1964
"A COSMOLOGY WITHOUT A COSMOS"

"WHAT do you think of Teilhard de Chardin?" In all the lectures which I have given on evolution across the country in the last two years, I cannot remember a single occasion on which this was not among the very first questions proposed for discussion. The impact of evolution on the several levels of human experience simply cannot be discussed without mentioning his name among the foremost contributors to the problem. I have rarely designed my lectures with a complete treatment of his work because I know that the question would be raised in discussion: "In all this, what part does the work of Teilhard de Chardin play?" There is almost no group, no discipline, no area of influence which has not made an attempt to hear what he has to say. Among intellectuals he is slighted only by a handful of men who are tightly held in the grip of anti-Teilhardian propaganda and cliché. There are those who create, who sweat and toil and produce the work, and there are always the sidewalk superintendents who leisurably lean on the fence, watch and comment.

It is always incredibly easy to reflect and comment upon the life work of another man. This is especially true of those who have never mustered the energy and ingenuity to engage in any public form of intellectual controversy. The matter would simply be pitiful or laughable if it were not for the fact that censorship within the Christian theological tradition, whether it be in the form of reviewing, reporting, journalism or classroom teaching, still has the power of cutting off a man's life work and delivering his final years to the melancholy of failure. Such was the effect of irresponsible censorship on Father Teilhard. Had he been allowed to explain and to clarify, to defend and develop his thought, rather than to suffer in silence, the community of searchers for insight and enlightenment would have profited enormously. It was a foolish and wasted martyrdom.

Now that we are well into the second half of the century, long after this great man's death, we are beginning to see the basic issue more clearly. It is not without deep reasons that in spite of the difficulty of reading Father Teilhard's writings (a difficulty which is compounded in translation), he remains on the lips of the educated man everywhere. This is doubly significant in that the name Pierre Teilhard de Chardin is itself an uncommon project of pronunciation for an American. The fact that anticipates his greatness is the unlimited praise and affection he has from every quarter of the intellectual community, despite creed, professional occupation or philosophical orientation. Men like Arnold Toynbee, Sir Julian Huxley, Theodosius Dobzhansky, Loren Eiseley, Graham Greene, Anne Fremantle, Michael Polanyi, James Collins, Karl Stern, Ashley Montagu—just a handful of the growing parade of his admirers—not only extol his efforts in bringing science, the humanities, philosophy and the Christian faith into harmonious dialogue, they prophesy his enduring greatness in the world of thought.

It would be a tempting abandonment of humility to ponder

why this is so, as if the mystery of human greatness could be plumbed by human reasons. Surely, there is involved here something of the divine madness of which Plato speaks in the *Phaedrus*. But one fact is clear. Teilhard de Chardin is a touchstone of our age. His life, his personality, his work, his thought, interpret for us something of the meaning of the past, and lift a tiny corner of the veil of the future. Over one hundred years of evolutionary study have been completed, and he has contributed original research in the fields of pale- ontology and physical anthropology. But what he has done for Christian philosophers and theologians in this area of physical origins is inestimable. Those who breathe easily about evolution today, as if it were "old hat," easily forget that within their own lifetime the "evolution of man" was still an objectionable phrase which seemed contrary to *Genesis* and the traditional philosophy and theology of the Catholic Church. What is more, they might easily forget that they possess a confidence and security today largely because Father Teilhard spent the greater share of his life in exile: exile from his Order to which he was ever faithful; from his Church which he loved with undying devotion; and from the intel- lectual and spiritual community of men for whom he gave his life's energy and genius. For this forgetfulness, it is salutary that we do penance, lest the same blindness strike again in our midst.

Looking back, now that the dust has settled, now that the people of God so enthusiastically claim him as their hero, now that the new General of his Order has reinstated him as a loyal brother and a giant among the research thinkers of our times, we understand better what has happened. He was living and working and thinking during those years between the early statements about evolution by the Holy Office, in 1909, and *Humani generis,* in 1950. For that half century, an article or a book on evolution, especially as the scientific studies touched upon human emergence, was rare. The reason was that until Pope Pius XII relegated the statements of the Holy Office about physical origins to the status of historical interest, the organic origin of man was not an open question in theological circles.

Although sometimes annoying, this gradual growth in theological development is normal and, understandably, slow. The same thing had happened in scriptural scholarship during that same era, a development which played no little role in the acceptance of evolutionary theory. Father Marie-Joseph Lagrange, a Dominican biblical scholar, was requested to stop writing, and to retire from one area of scholarly research in 1903, because he had introduced some very novel principles of secular historical interpretation into biblical studies. It was not until Pope Pius XII issued his encyclical *Divino Afflante Spiritu,* in 1943, that Father Lagrange came to be recognized as the father of contemporary Catholic biblical interpretation. The very principles for which he was opposed by suppressive ecclesiastical measures in 1903 have become key ideas to a more profound understanding of the Bible, to liturgical renewal, to the harmonious integration of contemporary science and culture with Christian spiritual life. It is becoming clear that authoritative censorship carries with it the lethal germ of unenlightenment, so destructive of the spiritual solidarity of the people of God. Neither Father Teilhard nor Father Lagrange lifted a finger of complaint, for they were magnanimous enough to see that their work would one day bear great fruit. But our understanding today, in the light of the discussions of Vatican Council II, has come too late for those countless men who ended their days tasting the bitterness and frustration of imposed silence.

But we are catching on. We are learning to guard against the hasty falling inflection, the unnecessary package deal, the narrow tribal mentality. In 1938, Pope Pius XI was asked by his theological advisors to use his authority to put an end, once and for all, to the "insidious" doctrines of physical and cultural evolution. To his great credit, and to our edification —for this was in 1938—he is reported to have replied: "One Galileo case in the Church is enough." Father Teilhard's lifetime work, like that of so many others like him, has taught us to open doors and windows, and to take care not to close them precipitously.

The spirit of Father Teilhard, however, does not merely hover about the mistakes and shortcomings of the past. His vision was ever one of building the future, and undoubtedly it is this courageous forward gaze, in the face of constant personal opposition, which so inspires the contemporary mind and heart. Now, at the end of Vatican Council II, we see realized so many of the things for which he stood. The age of blundering and incompetent censorship is ending, and slowly the idea that the normal, natural, professional dialogue which soberly evaluates men's thoughts and work assures a more enlightened balance. The way of critical refinement and correction which is invaluable to business enterprise, to professional endeavors, to scientific research, is equally valuable in philosophical and theological inquiry. This attrition is most valuable because it protects the freedom, the creativity, the integrity and rights of the human person.

Let us grant all this: that Father Teilhard is a touchstone of the times, that his contribution to evolutionary theory has been great, that he suffered a continuous injustice which has robbed us of a personal development of his vision, that his example may be the last martyrdom of inept censorship in a Church which has at last opened itself to the twentieth-century spirit. The question remains: What do *you* think of Teilhard de Chardin? What do you think of his vision, the vision of *The Divine Milieu, The Phenomenon of Man, The Future of Man* and his letters?

I would have to say that as Father Teilhard points to the world of reality and describes what he sees, I simply do not see it. What is obvious and indisputable to him because it is the very orientation of his personal experienced contact with the universe, with men and with God, is, to me, not obvious nor indisputable at all. Now I am not talking about Father Teilhard's factual backgrounds in scientific evolution; these points must be assessed separately by the men in the field. I am not talking about his dialectical method, nor his inferences, the rigor and consistency of which must be assessed by competent philosophical analysis, point by point. I am not talking about his theological foundations nor his fundamental religious beliefs. It can be supposed, contrary to those amateur theologians who set themselves up as self-appointed judges, that he is entirely orthodox from beginning to end. I am referring exclusively to what Father Teilhard insists are pristine phenomena, evidently open to all, obvious to anyone who will take the pains to see. Long before he reasons, develops inferences, argues his case, builds his vision, he points to reality and describes what he sees. I have strained my eyes along the sweep of his arm into the cosmic distance. I just cannot see what he says he sees.

Nor is this surprising. In matters of "either you see it or you don't," the field in which the treasure of every man's first principles is buried, there is reality, on the one hand, and the light by which he comprehends reality on the other. What a man sees is largely dependent upon his orientation, his point of view, the cast of his primal intuitions. Perhaps this is the reason why the speculations of Father Teilhard have never intruded seriously upon my own evolutionary reflections. I did not begin to read him until long after my own philosophical views of evolution were formulated. What is even more germane to the issue, our backgrounds and approaches to the world of reality are entirely diverse. Father Teilhard came to philosophy and theology through professional evolutionary science; although I had some background in field biology (animal ecology) and anthropology, my serious approach to evolutionary science came through professional philosophy. In evolutionary theory, Father Teilhard was born and raised in the tradition of Chevalier DeLamarck; my apprenticeship in evolutionary theory was at the feet of Simpson, Dobzhansky and Mayr, that is to say, in the tradition of Charles Darwin. I came into Roman Catholic belief through non-belief during mature days in the University; he approached non-believers from a long life of devout Roman Catholicism. As a priest formed in a religious tradition, he was a Jesuit; I am a Dominican. In philosophical

118

orientation, Father Teilhard was enamored of the insights of Henri Bergson; my deepest devotion is to Aquinas.

This tremendous diversity of orientation towards natural and supernatural realities makes all the difference in the world. It explains, in large part, why the strange world of Father Teilhard appears to me illusory. What seems to me to be the basic illusion in his vision is this: When Father Teilhard looks out (and inward) upon reality, he sees everything, without exception, as part of an orderly, harmonious whole. I just do not think that is the way the truth of the matter stands. I will briefly consider two examples which lie at the heart of Father Teilhard's vision: the cosmos and Christ.

Father Teilhard saw unity wherever he looked. To him, it was obvious and open to every serious observer that matter was one, that physical and spiritual energy are one, that the supernatural communion of human spirits is one, that the evolutionary processes throughout the universe are one, and that even science and religion are but the "conjugated phases of the same act of complete knowledge." For him, all reality is incredibly one; the reason the human understanding misses this, he thought, is that when man looks out upon reality, he concentrates upon the differences which, to him, are superficial. Total matter is one. It is impermissible, he tells us in *The Phenomenon of Man,* to break off a fragment and study it apart. The universe is a "gigantic atom," and by reason of the "unimpeachable wholeness of the whole," it is "a system, a totum and a quantum: a system by its plurality, a totum by its unity, a quantum by its energy; all three within a boundless contour."

119

For Father Teilhard, physical and spiritual energy are, somehow, a single energy. It is, he says, "depressingly and magnificently obvious," that all spiritual (human) endeavor involves physical activity, and vice-versa. There can be no doubt whatever, he asserts, that "there is something through which material and spiritual energy hold together and are complementary. In last analysis, somehow or other, there must be a single energy operating in the world." Even the supernatural activities of man are one. Speaking of the Eucharistic communion, he says: "All communions of a lifetime are one communion; all the communions of all men now living are one communion; all communions of all men, present, past and future are one communion. Have we ever sufficiently considered the physical immensity of man, and his extraordinary relations with the universe, in order to realize in our minds the formidable implications of this elementary truth?"

Finally, by an irreversible coherence of all that exists, "the least molecule is, in nature and in position, a function of the whole sidereal process, and the least of the protozoa is structurally so knit into the web of life that, such is the hypothesis, its existence cannot be annihilated without *ipso facto* undoing the whole network of the biosphere. The *distribution, succession and solidarity of objects are born from their concrescence in a common genesis* [his italics]. Time and space are organically joined again so as to weave, together, the stuff of the universe."

To assume so orderly and harmonious a cosmos that the world of matter, of spirit, of supernatural life, of evolutionary epigenesis responds to the rhythm of the same heartbeat is, to say the least, a magnificent hypothesis. But to say that the existence of this unity of the cosmos is obviously evident to anyone who would take the trouble to look, is, I think, a magnificent illusion. As a matter of fact, one could go further to say that to many twentieth-century intellectuals, the assertion of cosmic harmony, a total system of matter, spirit and Christian faith, is the medieval system in modern dress. To these it is a mythical anthropomorphism that must be exorcised from any realistic understanding of man's world. What precisely is *not* known is how far the theories of light and gravitation can be extended in time and space; unalterable, absolute laws of nature are not known to exist. Local cosmogonies affirm the interrelationship of our planet, the atmosphere, the stratosphere, the ionosphere within the solar system. But, as men like R. A. Lyttleton and G. J. Whitrow insist, "our idea of the universe as a whole remains a product of the imagination." Indeed, the structure of science rests upon the assumption of the applicability of cosmic laws and theories. If, then, we are to assert only what we know, what we can see at present, no such cosmic harmony and whole exists in the world of matter, let alone in the world of psyche, spirit and the supernatural.

What is far more obvious to me is the disorder, the waste, the hectic disorganization of the fragments of the universe of reality. It is painful to our age, but I am confident that the old idea of cosmic harmony is an illusion which has irrevocably collapsed. It may not necessarily be a "sickness unto death," nor a cause for "nausea," nor a final agnostic anxiety, but it is a point of realism that the universe of matter, of man and divine influence have been shattered and fragmented. We must rather start from this startling and undigestible fact. At

121

least this must be said: When I look out (and inward) upon the world of reality, this is what is obvious and unimpeachable to me: The universe may, in point of fact, *be one;* when God looks upon the universe He may *see it to be one;* but when I look out upon the universe of matter, of man and of God's handiwork, *I do not see it as one.*

The second exercise in "seeing" is similar to the first, yet, to me, it is far more illusory. It is the way the crucified Christ appears in Father Teilhard's vision, the key to the grand synthesis of *The Phenomenon of Man* and the spiritual doctrine of *The Divine Milieu.* With a swift and sure act of divine faith, he not only places Christ firmly within the universe of creatures, but also makes Him, through the inspiration of St. Paul, the meaning, the purpose, the fulfillment of the entire genesis and unfolding of creation. He is the One by which all things hold together. But what of the Cross, the crucifixion, the crucified Christ? For Father Teilhard, the Cross is the symbol which initiates the agonizing flight from sensible reality, the act of supernatural faith. The "folly of the Cross" is the request of God for man to stake his goods in the total Beyond. But this paradoxical request, though excessive, is not unexpected. In the words of Father Teilhard, ". . . that agonizing flight from the experimental zones—which is what the Cross means—is only (as should be strongly emphasised) the sublime aspect of a law common to *all* life." The Cross is the way of universal progress of evolutionary unfolding, of "human endeavour supernaturally righted and prolonged."

Now there is no hint of mere evolutionary humanism here. Father Teilhard is in no way suggesting that the coming of

Christ and His redemptive act is *necessitated* by the evolutionary design. He is fully aware that the meaning of the Cross cannot be suspected, much less comprehended, without an act of belief in the Judaeo-Christian revelation. To me, the only question is whether Father Teilhard gives full value to the contradiction, the intrusion, the absurdity (to use Kierkegaard's term) of the Incarnation, Death and Resurrection of Christ. Can one listen to Christ's repeated insistence that most men, even among those closest to Him, had missed the point of His coming, and still fit Him into a vision as the expected One?

It is easy to understand that in the world of science there is nothing so disturbing as an intruding divinity, a pocketful of miracles. Science has battled throughout its history to purge itself of the blight of myth, superstition and theological tyranny. When the anthropologist and the theologian sit around the same table in dialogue today, they must strive for at least a minimum of intellectual solidarity. A way must be found, a lexicon must be created, whereby the explanation of the emergence of the spirit of man does not jar with the evolutionary account of his physical origins. To bring the creative action of God into the picture as a kind of miraculous intrusion is the very thing that gives the scientist an uneasy feeling. There must be a more satisfactory way to explain the relation of matter and spirit in the genesis of man, and Father Teilhard's lexicon of phenomenological language may go far to overcome the impasse created by the demands of traditional philosophical terms.

On the other hand, it seems to me that the way Christ comes into a man's vision of reality is a consideration of an entirely different order. From its beginnings, the Judaeo-Christian revelation is an account of *magnalia Dei,* a succession of Divine intrusions. And Christ is *the* Intruder par excellence. On every page of the Gospels, Christ presents Himself to man as an inescapable datum face to face with which he must make up his mind. But what causes "fear and trembling" about that decision, as Kierkegaard profoundly underscores, is that the Cross of Christ is an event decisive in history. In every personal biography, it is a divine action of cosmic importance which overturns the universe. Christ never lets us forget that He constitutes an order absolutely apart; he chides those closest to Him for their failure to grasp His meaning even after He had been so long with them. Christ revealed Himself in terms of the absurdity of the Cross, which, as St. Paul admitted, was a "scandal to the Jews" and "folly to the Greeks." Hence, I find Father Teilhard's incorporation of the crucified Christ into his vision as merely symbolizing "the agonizing flight from the experimental zones . . . , a law common to *all* life" a completely unacceptable theological understatement. In short, the Christosphere of *The Phenomenon of Man* belongs to the illusion of the concentric; Christ reveals Himself as the eccentric, the Lord not of the expected order, but the Lord of the Absurd.

Many of the admirers of the vision of Teilhard de Chardin have chided me about my basic rejection of these two "obvious and unimpeachable facts," the cosmic unity and harmony of all things, and the Cross interpreted as a sublime aspect of the progressive evolutionary law of all life. They have suggested that my trouble may arise from two possible sources. First, perhaps I am unconsciously objecting to Father Teilhard's vision because it is so different from the Thomistic synthesis. Second, perhaps Father Teilhard's world is too futuristic, too advanced an idea to satisfy our age. Quite the contrary. My chief opposition to the vision of Father Teilhard is that it resembles far too much the Thomistic synthesis, and that it is, basically, too archaic to satisfy the demands of our contemporaries. The trouble with the world of Father Teilhard, as I understand it, is not that it is strange, but that it is not strange enough.

There is an enormous distinction which must be drawn between the *insights* of Thomas Aquinas and the *system* which has come to be known as Thomism. The insights of St. Thomas are magnificent realistic flashes of illumination which lay open a tremendous range of experience, cosmic, human and divine. Like the authentic insights of every other great thinker, man will never allow these gifts to be lost. But the system, the pedagogical blueprint, that St. Thomas drew up for the purposes of an age of scholasticism, has needed constant revamping from the first day of publication. The manual tradition of Thomism has not done its homework. The invaluable insights have often been obscured by uncritical and useless accretions. It is the *system,* the demands of the cosmic order and the order of knowledge, into which all things known and all things knowable must fit, which I find so unrealistic and illusory. The day of the "grand system" is over, and it is this quality of Father Teilhard's vision which so distresses me. His penchant to see all things one, to systematize the cosmos, the life of man, the revelation of God into a blueprint into which everything neatly fits, is far too much like the weakest aspect of contemporary Thomism: the monolithic organon.

Thus, Father Teilhard's vision is only futuristic in appearance; the old hankering for system, for deterministic order is still there. We are no longer looking for a system; we are looking for fragmentary insights which are realistic. The vision of tomorrow must be—if we listen to the youth immersed in the spirit of the contingent and the timely—truly historical. My tomorrow must have a value in itself. Yet Father Teilhard's vision seems to have all the qualities of the old myth of the eternal return, in which history is really incidental and novelty is, at bottom, only apparent. In his cosmic order, even Christ the Lord of history finds His "place" at the center, and the contradiction of the Cross is quite logical and expected. In that world, there is no terror, no trickery, no trouble—because there is no tomorrow. The God of the strange world of Father Teilhard is not the one I have come to believe in. His is the God of the neat; mine is the God of the messy. His God governs with unerring efficiency; mine provides with inexcusable waste. His God is impeccably regular; mine is irresponsible. His God is the Lord of order; my God is the Lord of the Absurd.

IX. NOTRE DAME

A Touch of Atheism

The twentieth-century intellectual is extremely uneasy with the traditional picture of Divine order and harmony in the world. For him, little remains of the old idea of cosmic order. St. Thomas's confidence in the "way things really stand" has resulted in a view of reality which is strange and mysterious: not at all the "mirror of Divinity" that his researches seemed to reveal. But this eventuality probably would not have taken St. Thomas by surprise. In fact, he refused to complete his "Summa Theologica" because of his own inner experiences with the world of reality and the presence of God. "I can write nothing more: all that I have hitherto written seems to me nothing but straw." Tradition usually interprets this statement to be the result of the transforming sublimity of his mystical favors. Yes, but what was it that he was allowed to see that so humbled his life's work? Josef Pieper, in his thoughtful book "The Silence of St. Thomas," suggests that he was manifesting openness to development, and that this remark "surely indicates that its fragmentary character belongs to the total implication of the 'Summa Theologica.'"

One might go further. It is quite consistent with St. Thomas's remarkable realism and mystical love of Christ to realize that the neat "cosmos" of the Greeks was a bit too perfect, too rationalistic, to endure the weight of empirical scrutiny and the mystery of the Cross. The basic contradiction of the Cross of Christ (which was foolishness to the Greeks) and the exaggerated cosmic order of Greek traditions might have so illumined this mystic as to convince him that he had built a house of straw. After all, this startling, blinding illumination had totally transformed the lives of St. Augustine and St. Paul before him. Order is tremendously

127

satisfying, but when a man is confronted with the "sickness unto death" it's not something you can believe and hope in. To a mother whose tiny child has just died of cancer, the suggestion that, in spite of all, the celestial spheres still sing in cosmic harmonies, has the consolation of a mouthful of ashes.

LECTURE AT THE UNIVERSITY OF NOTRE DAME, 1965
"ST. THOMAS AND THE HOUSE OF STRAW"

"No one really loses his Faith; he just stops living by it." These words, spoken by Bernanos's country priest, are filled with light, and they often return to me. Rarely do I lecture on a Catholic College campus without finding a group of students who will ask me, "In your discussions on the secular campus of state universities, do you run into much atheism and unbelief?" And these students are always baffled, if not scandalized, by the reply I usually give: "About as much as I find on the Catholic College campus." They seem to think that discussing evolution at a public university is like selling beer in Chicago: sooner or later you are bound to tangle with the Syndicate. Part of the confusion is generated by the old idea of the "religious" school and the "secular" school. Secular, for many, still means worldly (*in saeculo*), and the term "worldly" has numerous connotations: pagan, unbelief, agnosticism, atheism. The other aspect of confusion is a mistaken notion of atheism. Atheism is not organized unbelief, like a crime syndicate. It is more like the air we breathe. Unbelief comes up with the morning sun; it is mixed with our laughter and lurks behind the cynicism of the twinkling stars. If atheism is syndicated, we all have a membership card.

When a student thinks of atheism, especially in conjunction with a discussion about the evolution of man, the formidable image of Sir Julian Huxley (and his grandfather Thomas) comes to mind. Sir Julian's atheism is dramatic because he has chosen to become today's herald of a religion without revelation. Like Ezekiel, who walked about with broken pottery balanced on his head, you could hardly miss him. But when you come down to listening to Sir Julian's preaching, you are struck by two things. First, he is a remarkably religious man, in the authentic sense of "piety." Second, he is concerned with showing that you don't need God for the reasons usually given by Christians. It is a vulgar error not to take atheism seriously, wherever you find it. A zealous, perhaps even fanatic preoccupation with cutting away the impurities which infect the religious aspirations of man can be understood and even praised. To say that we don't need to overeat in order to cure anxiety neuroses is not the same thing as to say that we don't need food to exist. The point here is not to settle Sir Julian's problem, but rather to take a more realistic view of the complexity of unbelief.

We are all moving constantly in and out of various stages of unbelief. Ever since Augustine made the observation, Christian spiritual writers have distinguished levels of religious belief: *Deo credere, Deum credere, in Deum credere.* It is one thing to believe *that God exists,* another to believe *that He has spoken* audibly to man, and still another *to live by* what He has said. In the full and perfect commitment of belief, which places all hope and love, indeed a man's very existence, *in* God, these are not three isolated movements of the spirit. But anything less than this rare, pure aspiration

129

and practical commitment, which often involves much sacri-
fice and suffering, indicates that a man is involved in some
level of unbelief. He may, at times, be touched by the icy
finger of atheism.

Let us briefly consider the man who accepts the teaching
of Christianity and regards himself as a believer—and is so
regarded by others. It may take years before he discovers the
truth about the quality and motive of his Christianity. He
may discover that he accepts the teachings of Christ because
they are courageous and profound, that they are psycho-
logically sound and in tune with the finest sociological and
cultural studies. He may accept the tenets of Christianity because they have a remarkable interior coherence and unity,
and that they fit his speculations on the mystery of the
universe. Only a crisis would make him aware that his belief
was collapsing, and that he did not really believe Christ's
teaching for the only reason which could make him truly
Christian. Belief *in Christ* means to accept His words as true
because He is God. No lesser witness and warranty for the
truth of Christian doctrine suffices for authentic Christian belief, yet how many would be prepared to cast the first stone in
the direction of the unbeliever? The unbelief of the ordinary
man is undramatic, but he should take a good look in the
mirror before he stands up to accuse the atheist of unbelief.

The atheistic humanism of Huxley, the "provisional
atheism" of Sartre, and even the systematic atheism of Communism must be carefully reassessed in the light of the levels
of human unbelief. The crude idea that Communists are a
highly organized group of intellectuals who "don't believe in
God" is not merely uncritical, it is erroneous. To say that one

of the basic principles of Communism is atheism is like saying that one of the basic principles of democracy is freedom. It leaves too many things unsaid. The United States is a democracy, but daily bloodshed in the streets of the South reminds us that there remain some not so inconsiderable differences among us as to who shall enjoy freedom. Not all Communists have embraced atheism with equal commitment and enthusiasm. As with the idea of freedom in America, some Communists are only slightly "touched" by the notion. With the same serious caution must one approach the problem of "anxious atheism" wherever it is found, whether in the works of Sartre, of Merleau-Ponty, of Sir Julian Huxley.

When this is done, like the turning of the coin upon examination, we are rewarded with an insight into the positive value of unbelief, if one can so speak. Much of intellectual atheism today is postulatory, that is, an hypothesis which is used as a method, an instrument of clarification—pruning shears. If we were to compare the approach to reality of the tradition, say, of Thomas Aquinas, with that of a contemporary philosopher like Sartre, we would find that Aquinas viewed reality by means of a triple-faceted outlook: openness to Divine illumination; attention to the trans-historical and the permanent; the changing cosmos in space and time. His orientation was towards the timeless and the Divine. But Sartre, and our age, are suspicious about the tradition's apparent unconcern for the timely, the historical situation, the space-time contingency of existence. To prune the fruitless stubs and cancerous growths of this illusion, Sartre applies very sharp shears indeed. There is one way to be sure that we give a correct phenomenology of man's existence in his historical situation without undue influence of "the timeless and the Divine." Take as your first postulate: God does not exist. If you want to discover whether St. Anthony is responsible for finding golf balls, begin looking for your ball with the assumption that St. Anthony does not even exist. His proper role, the argument runs, can be assigned only by showing that golf balls can be found by anyone simply by looking in the right place.

The value of atheism today is to call attention to the many notions about Divinity and the timeless, having little foundation in the reality either of the cosmos or of revelation, but which have been passed along by tradition and which influence our interpretation of the present condition of man. In the name of a theological tradition, world-views, moral codes, psychological and sociological systems and behavior patterns have been imposed upon our age. This intrusion, many argue, has made Christian revelation virtually inaccessible to much of the world. Identification of the habits of the powerful aristocracy with "natural law" and Divine sanction was one of the scandals which precipitated the French Revolution and the tremendous wave of unbelief from which Western Europe never recovered. It is that precipitous identification of cosmic systems, moral and cultural views, psycho-social habit patterns, with the eternal Divine Plan, that, instead of assisting and insuring religious belief, ultimately stifles and uproots it. Atheism, aside from what it loses, forces the mind to see precisely what is to be *known* by interrogating the timely, and what is to be *believed* about the Divine. It is a bolt of atheistic lightning which has cleared the air today, and shows again what we should have known so well: Christ belongs to no culture, no age, no metaphysical system, no cosmology. He is subject to no psychological theory, no political plan, no economic group. Any attempt to prepare a man by this identification misses the whole point of the leap of the spirit into belief. Twentieth-century atheism has done Christianity a great service, one which the Fathers of Vatican Council II have recognized in approaching the delicate question of the role of the Church in the world. That service is to rid us of premature and cheap apologetics, of an overly anthropomorphic belief in God.

But the deeper and darker side of the cloud of unbelief which hovers over us has to do with what is lost by the postulate of atheism. Unfortunately, man does not live by theoretical postulates and hypothetical assumptions. He must have an ideology, a set of practical maxims which rule his choices, inspire his creativity, inflame and guide his loves, give meaning to his joys and sorrows, grace his energies with enough courage for death. To try to find meaning to live by in the world of the timely without the orientation of the timeless and without openness to the Divine, results in spiritual pathology, anxiety and a frightful "nausea" which debilitates and incapacitates man. Postulatory atheism has become less a denial and more the unbelief of *inattention* towards Divine things. But just as failure to be attentive dissolves the personal love and confidence and communion in a human friendship, so is inattention ultimately destructive of openness to the Divine. What begins as a theoretical postulate may end in practical disaster, especially when whole areas of reality are closed off to the heart and mind by the unswerving habit of looking the other way.

It is not that our age is, by nature, an incredulous one. We live as much by belief today as ever before. Though we admire the accomplishments of science and technology, the backdrop of twentieth-century life is belief, not scientific evidence and inference. We readily accept a given matter as real and true on the testimony of others whom we regard to be reliable and trustworthy witnesses. We do not question the quantum theory or relativity, but our assurance is based upon confidence in the testimony of professional experts. Scientists themselves openly and unashamedly reveal the beliefs which, unproved and undocumented, lie behind their scientific work. A case in point is the now famous letters which Einstein wrote to Max Born in which he confessed that although quantum physics and indeterminism had gained much ground, he could not believe that "God plays dice with the universe."

Nor does our age have trouble with the qualities of belief. To have certainty in matters alien to one's specialty, one's experiences, is quite acceptable. That our thinking be based upon the love and understanding of other persons (for the basis of belief is a loving confidence in another person) is distinctively contemporary. Karl Jaspers, for example, claims that belief links man with the ground of being, that it is the foundation of all our thinking and the indispensable source of all genuine philosophizing. That man can have certain basic insights into reality that are grounded upon a free, trustful, loving, personal acceptance of another's testimony is fully acceptable in our intellectual milieu today. The question for our times is one of *religious belief*. To believe something because someone has said it is not difficult for contemporary man. It is only when that someone on whose testimony the religious believer is asked to believe is God Himself that modern unbelief begins to ask: How is this possible to accept the claim that God has spoken in audible speech which man can hear and believe in? This is not a simple analogy, an easy step. It is, or seems to be, an unprepared leap into the dark.

Religious belief is mysterious but natural. In the face of the contemporary complaint that the demand to believe in Divine communication can hardly be justified, it seems fruitless to reply that, in reality, it is unbelief that does violence to the deepest fibres of man's being. Thomas Aquinas may have been inattentive to the details of the timely, but his instinct on this point was unerring. He saw the consequences of creatureliness, the unfinished existence of the cosmos, and the necessary receptivity of being. All was leaning so hard on nothing, at the opposite pole from self-possession and sufficiency. Above all, the spiritual creature, man, unfinished in choice, freedom, creativity and personal aspiration is open to the Divine. For Aquinas, not to recognize this necessary and natural openness, to close off the spirit by habitual indifference or inattention, was not only impious, it was a lethal, violent blow to man's existence itself. Failures in matters of the timely can be rectified by a better phenomenology—by taking a better look. But the folly of closing off the spirit of man to the Divine was, for Aquinas, a clumsy, blind, irrational piece of futility which could only end in illusions of the worst kind. In the presence of Someone who speaks, for a creature to remain passive and neutral, without attention and homage, this folly can be fatal.

On the other hand, it is not difficult to understand the uneasiness of our age about the consequences of "opening up to Divine communication." In our time, when freedom, creativity and interpersonal commitment are so much on our minds, we are well aware that not *any* openness to God is at issue. An impersonal God, who keeps the cosmic spheres majestically humming their celestial tunes, offers no trouble. A personal, subjective God who represents beauty, truth, goodness, tranquility, is, like a pastoral scene aesthetically satisfying and welcome. A life force, an *élan*, a spontaneous energy bursting forth in the evolutionary unfolding, is a God that adds dynamism and excitement but offers no problem. However, a God who is a Person, One who approaches us with understanding and love and communicates with us—this is, at first thought, terrifying. What if He should speak to *me*? I could never escape the consequences!

To be sure, there is no consolation to be drawn from the claims of the Judaeo-Christian revelation. What man is asked to believe is precisely what caused him to tremble as he stood on the threshold of belief. Constantly receptive of his very existence from moment to moment, open by nature and by necessity to Divine influence, he might have even expected God to speak to him. And God has spoken, in audible, comprehensible words, though in a most remarkable manner—as might have been expected.

To a handful of rather incompetent people, judged by the standards of the designers of great civilizations, He has entrusted a salvation history, an interpretation of the meaning of human existence, which reveals His assessment of the value of our today and our tomorrow. In and through the historical unfolding of this people, there is to take place a dramatic event of the most mundane yet mysterious kind—a life, a death, a resurrection—which will transform all of existence, time and space. In the face of this dramatic event, the man who remains open to the Divine communication will be asked to make a decision which will change the meaning of the cosmos, turn the universe, as it were, upside down. His Son, Jesus Christ, will enter that history and then appear *to all men* as an inescapable datum face to face with which each man must make up his mind. No reality will remain untouched by this event; nothing will be the same again.

*   *   *   *   *   *

Speaking as a person who came up from the depths of unbelief during the most energetic, intellectually active, spiritually self-critical days of young adulthood, I cannot think that questions of *content* of that Divine communication are impediments to believing *in God* today. Much attention, too, is paid to questions of the historical form of that revelation, the authentic interpretation of God's speech, and the relation of salvation history to world development and cultural unfolding. These are certainly important and difficult questions for the believer, and not a few men have found it impossible to believe in God's revelation because of the *way it is tied to cultural accretions,* to metaphysical systems and archaic world-views. The relations of God's people, those who have received with openness and love and expectation what God has said, to the world in which they plan and live their daily lives, must ever be an important concern for the Spirit of God. But I cannot be persuaded that it is at the central nerve of that atheism with which each of us is touched.

I think that it is rather the lack of openness to God which arises from the *growing inattention to Divine presence* which is the basic issue today. If the consequences of inattention are deadly—for there is only *one way* that Divine communication can open reality to the human spirit, and that is through free, personal receptivity of God's speech—then what is doubly serious is the impersonal attitude of the people of God towards the God who has spoken to them. I think that the future of atheism, of the unbelief of inattention (for how many deliberately refuse assent to a truth which one has recognized with sufficient plainness to be God's speech?), lies almost entirely in the hands of those who believe. They must make some dramatic sign that the personal God with whom they are communicating with love and confidence *is actually in our midst today*. They must account for the scandal of the "silence of God" and "His boundless muteness in these clamorous times." If your God is so personal, so close and so loving, so communicable and such a confidant, *then where is He?*

In short, we do not need a demonstration of God's existence today; we need a demonstration of His personal presence among us. Christ did not come to demonstrate His Father's existence, but to witness to His presence among us. Those who think that they have to establish an *ordo universi,* a great chain of causes, to introduce God to twentieth-century atheists, have not grasped the kind of unbelief into which we have become entrapped. We are *drama* people, not *picture* people.

A God of a harmonious cosmos, of aesthetic beauty, truth and goodness, of a great chain of causes, of finalities and vital forces, we do not need today. We don't need a God we can admire; we need a God we can believe in, one in whom we can place our trust and love. We need to recognize God personally present to us in our day, personally speaking to us. There is only one sign of personal, loving presence, and, though it may be hard to define or even describe, no one misses it. The face of a Teilhard de Chardin radiates it; the calm, peaceful confidence of a mother with her dying child in her arms reveals it; the courage of a march for rights proclaims it. Interpersonal attentiveness to the drama of His presence is the delicate demonstration of God for our times.

One might go even further and observe that any attempt to reinstate the traditional "proofs for the existence of God" as an antidote to contemporary unbelief is not only irrelevant, it may aggravate the malady and close the doors of the mind and heart more tightly. The result of extensive dialectical restatement of systematic metaphysical arguments would be to underscore what most men today suspect: that the Christian God is, like the Greek God, a distant, impersonal, detached potentate, who, if not totally indifferent to creation, sends an occasional message from time to time just to "keep in touch." These traditional proofs, no matter how they are tightened up logically and empirically, can never supply the personal influence which man so sorely needs. To underscore order, intelligence, power and finality today cannot possibly provide the symbol of a personal, loving God who communicates with us in our frustrations, misery, failures and disorders. After all, when the plant is running smoothly, who needs the superintendent? It is when the machine breaks down that his personal presence is required.

Ironically, it has been my experience that the only people who have any patience for and interest in the "demonstrations for the existence of God" are those who already believe in His presence. It almost seems like a chess game which is only indulged in by club members with a lot of leisure at their disposal. A few years ago, at the University of New Mexico, a group of very good students were offered a semester course in the philosophical analysis of the traditional proofs for God's existence. The professor was one of the best prepared instructors on this subject I know. At the termination of this excellent course, in which adjustment was made to update the lexicon and empirical facts about cosmic matter, energy, motion and order, the students reacted quite strangely. If the dialectics of the arguments were so intricate and the factual materials so difficult to grasp, they doubted, for the first time in their lives, if they could demonstrate the existence of God. Some few of the more confident intellectuals went so far as to doubt whether *anyone* could prove the existence of God. Of course, they all *believed* in the personal God of the Christian revelation.

No, I think that we must look elsewhere than into the realms of impersonal order, harmony and determined causes. He cannot be the God of organization, of chancery decrees and monitums issued from distant places, of manuals and rules, some kind of great scout master. He must be dramatically present among us, now. Here is the requirement of belief today: God must come among us and live with us and speak to us today. He must be personally present. That our days are filled with chaos and not celestial harmony is the condition. Let Him come and share this existence with me. It is not "pie in the sky" that I need, not another myth of the eternal return. I need a Lord of my history, a Lord of my todays and my tomorrows. Then can I love and trust. Then can I believe.

The Lord of the Absurd

There was an old lady
Who swallowed a bird.
It's so absurd . . .
To swallow a bird;
She swallowed the bird
Who swallowed a spider
That went blub-blub
Deep down in-side-her;
She swallowed the spider
Who swallowed the fly;
I don't know why
She swallowed the fly . . .

LECTURE AT THE UNIVERSITY OF CALIFORNIA IN BERKELEY, 1965
"THE LAND INTO WHICH DARWIN LED US"

SOONER or later, the discussion crosses the Rubicon of seriousness. Lately, the point is reached almost immediately. It is beautiful, yet a bit terrifying, to see how swiftly the human spirit moves out upon the threshold of mystery. My lectures on the evolutionary theme are always enjoyable—for all of us. The university communities are ever open toward this kind of issue, which is a bit controversial, partly scientific, partly philosophical, ever touching upon the theme of the human condition. They appreciate whimsies, are patient with technicalities, are willing to accept a point, debate a point, set a point aside. But just as soon as I work my way out upon the ledge of ultimate human belief, the audience becomes pensive, a bit anxious and disturbed. Then they resist, many of them. It is a benevolent resistance, but you can observe in the attentiveness, the clenched jaw, the lowered eyes, the slight shaking of the head, that the matter is not going down easily. And what is the bitter truth that is so hard to accept? Simply this: That a deeply penetrating look at the unfolding cosmos and the history of man reveals a world at odds with itself and a mankind in a desperate situation lacking every possible remedy. In short, man is hopelessly caught up in a monstrous absurdity—human existence.

Very well. But what do you mean by "absurdity?" That's the way it usually begins, and it's a good way. Absurd is a "harsh-sounding" word. There must be a way of softening it, of qualifying its use in this discussion. According to the dictionary, the word "absurd" commonly means "contrary to reason; obviously inconsistent with the truth, opinions generally held, or the dictates of common sense"; it also means "ridiculously incongruous." We do use the term in many ways, it is true. For example, the evolutionary unfolding of the universe, especially as it is revealed in the prehistory of the plants and animals on our planet, often manifests its incongruous side. P. G. Wodehouse refers to the mandrill as "an animal that wears its club colors in the wrong place." No one can contemplate the beak of the Brazilian caw-caw, the horn of the rhino, or the buck teeth of the wild boar without concluding that the Creator is a clown.

Then, too, there is the more serious side of the unfolding

universe which has always inspired man with awe. Scientific probing has not diminished the mystery of nature. On the contrary, the wonderful, the awe-full, the unbelievable strangeness of the universe is increased by each discovery. As we interrogate matter and peer into the submicroscopic particles and agents, determinism has given way to indeterminism. The blinding flash and deafening noise of the release of entrapped energy within the nucleus of the atom have forced us to stand back in terror. We feel less and less at home in the megaloscopic universe of metagalaxies and quasars, incomprehensible in size, countless in multitude, incalculably distant and rushing away at incredible speed. We may scratch the surface of the problem of life, we may appear to harmonize the paradox of matter and spirit, we may land a human space ship on the moon, and a thousand other wonders. But with each step, another, deeper, awesome strangeness will be uncovered.

These are the incongruities of the contemplative, the wonders which inspire surprise, delight and belly-laughs. Evolution is an unfolding filled with another kind of eccentricity: the clash of disorder, destruction and extinction. When we meditate upon the dynamic order which evolution has placed before us at this moment, we find it hard to believe that the main theme of the symphony is barely heard. Listen again, and it begins to emerge. Evolution of life, and the emergence of man, is a natural process in which chance, failure, waste, disorder and death will ultimately prevail. The entire destiny of the upsurge of life and all of its efforts have been enshrouded, from the beginning, by a cloak of "heat-death," which, one day, will cut off the source of life—the sun. The very air we breathe is drawn from a thin film of atmosphere which hovers precariously over the seas and mountains and prairies that have been pushed up for us to stand on.

If we take care to pay no attention to the fact, if we concern ourselves with the here and the now, the condition of evolutionary extinction, the rhythm of coming-to-be-and-passing-away lulls us into a sense of tranquillity. So the giant shy condor will soon become extinct. Too bad, but that's the way things are. But a larger order prevails and, as e. e. cummings says: "God's in His andsoforth." We are, of course, whistling ourselves a tune. The tune is supported by science which is based upon an assumed order of the cosmos, without which its laws and theories would be unpersuasive. The tune is supported, too, by the traditional philosophies of wheels within wheels, of cosmic harmonies set into celestial motion with the guarantee of eternal return. The tune is supported, finally, by the most enduring of theological myths which have, from the beginning, taken the terror out of history (and therefore evolution) by annulling the effect of time and space through deliberate forgetfulness. But listen more closely for the real motif. Could this not be the repeated illusion of mankind, the short-sightedness which has always tempted him to fall into idolatry?

Grand illusions sound their tocsin through the trumpets of little events. Absurdity attaches itself to the unlawful, and, like creaks in the attic, remains unnoticed for aeons of time. Few have ears to hear these sounds. However, no matter how antiseptic a man tries to make his life, he cannot avoid the tears out of which his most lasting joy is composed. No one escapes; yet each of us believes so eagerly that he can discover an exit. Instances of this paradoxical point abound in our lives, yet it is not easy to place our finger on the heartbeat of the issue, much less describe it to another. Absurdity rides on the backs of tiny events...

There is no place in North America more lovely in December than Boca Raton, Florida. Whenever the opportunity allows, I return to that Eden to retrieve lost strength from the ocean air, and to breathe again the youthful joy of being in the midst of my closest friends.

One day, while lying on the warm sand near a seaside *villa* where I was spending the afternoon, I was watching the blue-green Atlantic smash against the reefs below me and was following a great white cargo ship slowly disappear in the direction of Miami. At that very moment, my whole life, with all its collected meaning over the years, seemed to spiral upwards in an exhilarating movement towards the Boca sun. In a burst of enthusiasm, I shouted out that this was undoubtedly the most memorable moment of my life!

Not far away, two little beach waifs were playing in the sand, making tunnels to the ocean and laughing as the sea continuously washed them away. In their world, I'm sure that my outburst could have meant nothing. Yet one of them —the one who seemed always to smile whenever anything different came into view, and insisted upon singing a tune the words of which seemed to run "All by myself in the morning"—looked up in amazement. Her red-haired, freckled playmate, who was frolicking with a spotted Dalmatian much larger than herself, actually said, "Something big has happened?" Then she too laughed, and I immediately recognized the voice. It was the Lady of Sandia. As I was about to speak, I remembered the Sandia Crest, and how the Lady's visit into my meditations had had that power to gather my life from end to end into lucid meaningfulness. I feebly attempted to tell my young friends something about this flash of total joy, but as I spoke (quite incoherently) the little redhead turned away, threw sand in the direction of her dog, and her humming friend resumed her aimless song.

Then I noticed that the ship had disappeared into the Gulf; that the clouds began to obscure the Boca sun. The rising tide had brought the salt-sea spray farther up upon the shore, and it had a bitter tang. The fledgling sandpipers were nervously side-stepping the lash of the foaming breakers, lest they wet their feet. The thought of Sandia had brought with it a tremble, and I felt then how expensively man purchases his moments of joy. The inexorable tears would soon destroy the illusions that ever hover about all happiness; but the memory of such moments is our only promise of a paradise to be regained. It seems so absurd that this be the quality of the highest gifts of human happiness, yet we cannot have it otherwise.

Absurdity, as we best know it today through the novels and plays of Sartre, Camus, Ionesco and Beckett, belongs properly to the moral and religious order. It refers to the miserable condition into which all men are born and from which they cannot escape. The term "absurd" has entered existential literature through the meditations of Kierkegaard, but rarely does the theatre or the novel carry the analysis into the depths of Christian belief. Just short of this threshold, the theatre of the absurd is unceasingly pointing to the tragic element in the life of man, the paradox of a world at odds with man, which opposition can neither be changed nor tolerated. In lieu of all possible remedy, man has a single option: He may acquiesce, as did Gide, or he may revolt, as did Camus. In either case, the situation remains hopeless.

Back to the question: What do I mean by absurdity? All of the above meanings of the word can be verified in the evolutionary unfolding of man. The human situation, with all its incongruity, its frivolity and fate, its wonders and strangeness, its apparent meaninglessness, poses a dilemma for man. In sum, it means that life is difficult, man is pitiable; his courage is tried in a crucible of clay. There is still another meaning of the word "absurdity" which adds a dimension of infinite depth to the already insoluble issue. It is the absurdity of the Word which God speaks to man as he stands dazed and blinking before his incomprehensible dilemma.

Sir Julian Huxley is entirely correct to chide the Christians for yelping like frightened dogs in the face of misery which they could at least muster the courage and ingenuity to alleviate. There is a sense in which the too ready "Lord, Lord" makes cowards of us. It is, as Jean Daniélou remarks, "a monstrous abuse of Christ's atonement to make of it no more than a labor-saving device." In the evolutionary scheme, exclusively within the confines of which Huxley prefers to meditate, the survival of man depends upon courageous, free, personal, creative effort. Upon this remarkably simple interpretation of human existence, an entire morality, a complete spirituality (if the term may be so used) can be constructed. Indeed, such an ideology has been formulated by the evolutionary humanists.

Unfortunately, the absurdity of man's desperation is compounded by a wound which is far deeper and infinitely more deadly, a condition which the superficiality of the Marxist and humanist analyses fail to appreciate. It is not merely the evolutionary struggle that man is trying to survive. With a bit of courage, foresight and luck, he might be able to fashion a future to which he can adapt. But no matter how hard he tries, he cannot alter or palliate the wrath of the angry God. It is not until man is confronted with the dramatic event of Christ's Incarnation that, at last, he places his finger on the raw nerve of the real absurdity. Face to face with the Lord of the Absurd, man is asked the only authentic question: "Will you also go away?"

*   *   *   *   *   *

Reading the Christian account of salvation history as an outsider from the standpoint of secular cultural history, it is preposterous from the first page on. That God should single out a handful of disorganized, culturally incompetent, Jewish tribes, mould them into a people, and enter into their history by becoming incarnate, is unbelievable enough. That the incarnate God should suffer, die, rise from death and thereby literally change the meaning of cosmic existence must be looked upon, from outside the Faith, as a fabulous myth. But the question with which I am faced more and more in my reflections on the unfolding of man's existence is: Does the drama of the Incarnation, Death and Resurrection of Christ appear less absurd to the believer? Or, as the writings of Father Teilhard and others suggest, does Jesus Christ present

Himself as the God of order, emerging as the ruler of the harmonious, dynamic evolutionary epigenesis? Does He come as the expected one to the scientist, the philosopher, the wise man? Or does He come as an Intruder, the Uninvited Guest upsetting every expectation?

I cannot help but reveal my hand. Each time I return to this question of how Christ presents Himself to the decisive spirit as an inescapable datum, the wedge is driven more deeply between the world of cosmic law and the unforeseen intrusions of God. So crushing was the absurdity of Christ's coming into the world to those who first witnessed that visit, that, from the vantage point of the Cross upon which He met disaster, no man could tolerate His oppressive presence. They all went away. From that time until now, men slowly straggle back to Calvary, and He must repeat the same unbelievable story. Man has found a way to listen to this terrible tale, but he never gets used to it. How any man can find in Christ the Lord of cosmic order is totally beyond me. He has always presented Himself as the Lord of the Absurd.

Christ places himself fully within the revelation of the Old Testament. Not only is he the one whom the prophets predicted; he refuses to abrogate a single moral law given to the chosen people of God. However, he underscores from the outset that the utter hopelessness and despair of humanity is an irreparable moral and religious pathology which successive generations only aggravate. It is not just a natural property of evolutionary unfolding. It is the result of two deeply rooted attributes of human existence: *creatureliness* and *grievous moral fault*. Forgetfulness of creatureliness is the prelude to the fall into idolatry, and the theme of the Old Testament salvation history without which Christ's entry into the world cannot be understood is: God is angry.

Now the anger of God is not to be thought of as a passion for vindictiveness. This is far too anthropomorphic for the reality of religious commitment involved, a sentimentalism into which those people fall who find only fear in the Old Testament and love in the New Testament. Rather, the anger of God represents His intensity of being. "I am who am" is the name of God in the Old Testament, a name so sacred that it was seldom pronounced. This idea of God must not be forgotten if we are to grasp the sense of divine madness of the revelation. The Christian metaphysician is fond of saying that we know more what God is not than what he is. Yet more often than not, Martin Buber has observed, he speaks as though he knew what God is. The Old Testament revelation does not ask a man to make a speculative analysis of the analogy of being; it rather demands of the personal freedom of man that he abdicate everything in the presence of the anger of God, *that he practice creatureliness* in all its bitter humiliation.

A corollary of this spiritual exercise is the readiness of the people for the unexpected intrusions of God into their day, their history. The Old Testament is a collection of records of many centuries of Divine interventions, of *magnalia Dei,* a continual series of prophesies and miracles. These people of God were invited to draw near to God but they were never allowed to forget that He was surrounded by a burning bush. "No one sees God and lives." They were apprenticed in the habit of openness to God. This receptivity, however, was not untouched by terror, anxiety, by the ground of religious perplexity upon which the communion of creature and Creator had to be based. We often hear that God does not ask, nor expect, the impossible. The God of the Old Testament was incessantly asking the impossible. He came into the lives of the Jews in the oddest ways, at the oddest times, making the oddest demands.

In our generosity, we invite friends to come and visit "anytime at all"—just so long as they give us a day's notice. The chosen people were brought up to realize that it is impossible to prepare for the visit of God. Christ was to remind man of the old Jewish proverb: "You know not the day nor the hour . . ." The prayer of Habakkuk, the Song of the Children, and the Wisdom literatures are filled with the intrusions of God, not only into the life of man, but into the cosmic harmony of the universe. Only by little did the people of God come to know that the anger of God was a call of love, shaking them from slumber. How often had they cried out that their desolation might be traded for tranquillity. With such harsh contradictions was humanity prepared for what was to be the "hardest saying of all": the Incarnation of God into human history itself.

From the very beginning, Christ mirrored this sign of contradiction in which God's love and His anger are identical. Everything about Christ, when you come right down to it, was intrusive upon a world of order. What He said about His origins, about Himself, what He did, and what He expected of others was strange. Only His manner was disconcertingly gentle. He drew everyone to Him: children, drunkards, criminals, aristocrats, prostitutes, rulers, professional men, laborers, foreigners and displaced persons. He wept with friends and relaxed with idlers of the tavern. He accused no one, condemned no one—except to keep the records straight among the "religious" about the rights of the angry God. His quiet, friendly, loving, merciful, sympathetic way brought everyone near enough to see what He was about, to hear what He was saying, to receive a personal invitation to follow Him. But here is where the orderly and the gentle ends and the harshly unexpected begins. At once, when He reveals what this invitation entails, you sense the intrusion of the Divine once more.

Who is He and where is He from? You expect Him to say "Bethlehem" or "Nazareth." Instead, He speaks of coming from the Father, where He has dwelt long before there were cities of any kind. He tells of being sent by the Father, whom no one has seen but Him, with a message which no one knows but Him and those to whom He chooses to reveal its contents. He sounds a bit like the angry God Himself with his admonitions to be vigilant, lest God come upon them like a thief in the night. "When you least expect . . ." says this Intruder. He speaks of such familiarity with the Father that either he blasphemes or man's deepest religious understanding has to be revised. There are three Persons in the Godhead, not one: the Father whom they know; the Son who is revealing this hidden truth; and the Holy Spirit who was to come and make plain all that He now spoke in parables. He and the Father and the Spirit are One. What is more, if they wished to be victorious over the crushing misery of human life and inglorious death, they must believe in Him as they do in the Father, follow Him all the way to the death on the Cross. Every word was an intrusion, not only upon their humanity, but even upon their most sacred and hallowed religious traditions. Every word was contrary to their hopes and expectations. Every word was absurd.

Christ's invasion of the life of man went further than His words, which were true to the prophetic form of the *magnalia Dei,* the wonder-working of God. Just as His speech betrayed a disconcerting displacement of meaning to all ideals the Jews held dear, so now what He was doing manifested His intention to upset the cosmos and all its laws. He ruled His daily existence with miracles. He grasped space and time in His hands and set aside the laws of nature like a forgotten toy. Many men like to see in St. Paul's words that Christ is "the first-born of all creation, in whom and by whom all things exist and hold together" an inclusion of the Redeemer into the very structure of cosmic unfolding. What they fail to recall is that He did not hesitate to shake the cosmic frame to its foundations and turn it topsy-turvy at the slightest inspiration of Divine madness. Time and space are His, and there is no promise nor hope that the universe will continue to unfold with determined necessity—if it ever did. The scientist can count on the regular motions of the heavens and the philosopher can speculate upon order, but there is not the slightest expectation from the interpretation which Christ has given to His creation that man can rest the meaning of his tomorrow upon his cosmic harmony.

It is not simply that Christ performed miracles. These were just a prelude to the drama which must be placed alongside the events of creation and Incarnation in cosmic proportions and human significance. He voluntarily suffered, died on the Cross, and rose from the tomb, bringing redemption and eternal release to man—a creature entrapped in an intolerable and irremediable physical and moral condition. The absurdity of the evolutionary world of Huxley and the nauseating existence of Sartre touch only upon the creation and its mysterious misery. It is the cosmic act of Divine redemption which has really intruded upon man's existence and has transformed the universe of space and time. It is not only what Christ *said* that challenges our credulity, it is what He *did* that is unbelievable. Who can believe that God so loved man that He would die for him? This seems not only blasphemous; it seems patently absurd.

But it is what Christ *expects* of man which is the crushing blow. In trading the law of fear for the law of love, Christ changed the orientation of man's entire spiritual life. One thing He did not change. He, like the Father, still asks and expects the impossible. He expects a full-grown man, with all the vigor and sincerity of total personal commitment and ultimate decision, to abrogate his precious freedom in favor of entering into the drama of suffering and death—his Life. The man who has not yet heard this invitation clearly enough, or who is still too disjointed and personally disorganized to draw himself together in a single act of absolutely free decision, will not comprehend the terror, the finality, the irrevocable consequences of saying either "yes" or "no." One day, he will see clearly that no matter how terrifying are the prospects of decision, he can no longer turn away.

Perhaps it will come as it did to Peter.

It was one of those grey days, filled with grim skies and the metallic taste of confusion and bitterness. Christ has just made another of those statements: "Unless you eat my body and drink my blood, you shall not have life in you; he

155

who eats of my body and drinks my blood shall never see death." *Credis hoc?* Do you believe this? Peter must have had that sick feeling in his heart which Abraham felt as he walked towards Mount Moriah to obey God's command to kill his son Isaac. There was that old silence which always accompanied these awful moments. How can a man be expected to follow *this* man going *this* way? Had not God, the angry God, commanded him not to follow strange teachings? Had He not warned against the idolatry, the sacrilege and the blasphemy of pagan nature worshippers? Eating and drinking this man's body and blood! Even if there were a mystical meaning which would remove the vulgarities of cannibalism, it would mean venerating this man as the giver of eternal life—the prerogative of the One, True God. But what if, as He claims daily, He is God . . .

How far we are now from the ludicrous and the laughable, from the merely mysterious and paradoxical, from the chance and disorder of an evolutionary universe and from the apparent meaninglessness of human existence. These are minor absurdities, and the cries of men like Huxley and Sartre and Camus trapped in their impossible and intolerable situations, are like those of a child with a bruise compared to the groans of Peter as he watched the trusted friends and disciples shake their heads and leave at this "hard saying." Then he heard the question that struck terror into his heart, the last one he wanted to hear at this moment. "Will you also go away?" At the moment least prepared for, a man suddenly sees clearly the truth of the Divine madness and can no longer withhold his decision. Peter's answer is not enthusiastic, not generous, but in the face of the absurdity of following this man this

156

way, one has to swallow hard. "To whom shall we go? You have the words of eternal life." Against the dreary sky on that memorable day of another taste of ashes, Peter knew that he was looking into the eyes of the Lord of the Absurd. Half-hearted, slightly bewildered, his reply was good enough for a beginning. Another day was coming when he would have another chance at the question. This time, with his very life itself, he would be able to reply: "Lord, you know all things, you know that I love you."